THE UNIVERSITY COLLEGE OF RIPON AND YORK ST. JOHN

YORK CAMPUS

Please return this book
- if recalled, the

- 2 JUN 1999		RETURNED
- 8 MAY 2002	1 5 DEC 2006	0 3 MAY 2007
1 4 FEB 2003	3 0 SEP 2007	RETURNED
	RETURNED	1 9 MAR 2008
2 NOV 2003	2 4 JAN 2008	
	RETURNED	
	1 9 DEC 2008	
2 3 FEB 2006	2 0 MAR 2009	
0 5 MAY 2006		

CANCELLED

Fines are payable for late return

The Gospel Community and its Leadership

John Tiller
with
Mark Birchall

Marshall Pickering

Marshall Morgan and Scott
Marshall Pickering
3 Beggarwood Lane, Basingstoke, Hants RG23 7LP, UK

Copyright © 1987 by John Tiller and Mark Birchall
First published in 1987 by Marshall Morgan and Scott Publications Ltd
Part of the Marshall Pickering Holdings Group
A subsidiary of the Zondervan Corporation

British Library CIP Data
Tiller, John
  The gospel community.
  1. Church renewal
  I. Title
  262'.0017   BV600.2

ISBN: 0 551 01398 2
Phototypeset in Linotron Times
by Input Typesetting Ltd, London
Printed in Great Britain by
Guernsey Press Ltd, Channel Islands, UK.

336447

Contents

Preface

This book brings together two enterprises which have become so interwoven that each depends upon the other. My friend Mark Birchall has given a large part of his time over the past three years to investigating the way in which a remarkable number of churches belonging to a variety of denominations and traditions have begun to develop a corporate style of leadership. It seemed to me that the results of this research have a great significance for the church everywhere and I was concerned that they should be made available through publication. At the same time I was myself exploring the obstacles to renewal in the life of the historic denominations in this country. The questions in brief were whether, in response to spiritual movements in the churches in recent years, we could hope to reform sufficiently the existing institutional structures, whether we should create some additional structures, or whether we must inevitably resort to some completely new alternative structures.

Our two projects have come together in the vision of the 'gospel community'. We have asked what Jesus intended for the group of disciples whom he commissioned to be his witnesses. We have found in Scripture, not a single blue-print for church order (which would have soon become obsolete anyway), but a radical reinterpretation of the purpose of religious association. The problem for the church is not its age, but its preoccupation with the religion of the sanctuary, its concern for its own preservation, and its subjection to a professional ministry. All of these things can afflict à new church just as much as an old one.

It will be obvious from the way we write and the examples we quote that we are Anglicans. It is the Church of England which has shaped our experience in the main, and whose blemishes also we see most clearly. Nevertheless we have tried not to let our personal prejudices or frustrations control our thinking, and we have ranged very widely in the evidence we have considered. For convenience we use the word 'minister' to refer to the ordained leader of a local congregation of whatever denomination. Our thanks are due to those ministers who have willingly submitted to questioning about progress towards corporate leadership in their churches; to the staff of diocesan and denominational organizations who gave us contacts and other help; to Denise Carter, Jean Hamilton, and Joyce McSorley, who coped with Mark's inability to type; and to many others who have encouraged us to believe that this book can make a contribution to the renewal of the church. Most of all we are indebted to our wives and families, to whom we have demonstrated convincingly once again that the birth of a book creates more upheaval in the home than the birth of a baby!

We offer this work, not because we are particularly conscious of its originality, but because we are able to point to what others wiser than ourselves have been saying for the last twenty years, and also to what the Holy Spirit appears to be doing in all kinds of churches in all denominations. Our hope and prayer is that readers will be encouraged by our argument, and by the experience of others which we describe, to move toward appropriate patterns of corporate leadership in their own churches and to persevere, whatever the difficulties, until they can see that the whole body is being built up into that unity of faith, knowledge of Christ and spiritual maturity which is God's purpose for his church.

Scripture quotations are given, with permission, in the New International Version, copyright 1978 by the New York International Bible Society.

Part one: The problem

1: Can the churches be revived?

One hundred years ago the churches in Britain were on the crest of a wave. Between thirty and forty per cent of the population attended church on an average Sunday and the membership of most denominations was increasing more quickly than the rapidly expanding population. Extraordinary efforts were being made to build new places of worship for the people moving into the vast housing developments which were springing up in most towns. So vigorous were the attempts to reach the young that in some places there was hardly a child who was not either sent to Sunday school or taken to church.

The impact of Christianity on late Victorian Britain was certainly lessened by the fact that in the poorer parts of the big cities church attendance could be well below ten per cent. Even that, however, is impressive by modern standards, and the leaders of the Victorian churches were far less complacent than their successors today often appear to be about the unevangelized masses.

It is not a true generalization to say that the working classes never went to church. Churches and chapels in the northern and midlands manufacturing towns were often at the centre of close-knit communities, and the same could be said of the mining valleys of South Wales. Very few people denied having any church allegiance at all. A Liverpool census of 1881 discovered no more than 0.6 per cent of the population who did not belong to any Christian denomination, and this figure included some foreign seamen.[1]

The marked contrast to all this which confronts us today inevitably prompts questions about how the churches in Britain could lose so much of their appeal within the space of hardly more than a single generation. But the decline also raises the issue of whether a revival of Christianity is now possible. Could the picture be just as quickly reversed, or have the churches sunk to the point where they no longer possess the dynamism and the resources to undertake a nationwide mission? Must we accept that we are now a post-Christian society with a spiritual future which will be very different from anything we have known in the past?

The hope of revival

Some people believe that revival is just round the corner. At least the steep decline in churchgoing which occurred during the sixties has now slowed down. That in itself may constitute a very slender ground for hope, but it is possible to argue that the churches have now reached a condition where the nucleus of the truly committed believers is much more clearly identified. The very strength of Christianity in late Victorian times undoubtedly produced social pressures to conform, with the result that churchgoing became, at least for the better off, the respectable thing to do.

It would be foolish to pretend that group pressures no longer prompt people either to identify with or to dissociate themselves from their local church. Such influences can be very strong, for example in youth work, or through popular opinion of a rural vicar. But *belonging* to the church and *being* the church are beginning to receive greater emphasis than *going* to church. The question, 'Are you a Christian?' has received sharper definition in a hostile philosophical climate, and although the churches are slimmer numerically than they used to be it could be argued that they are in a healthier condition spiritually.

The changing climate

Furthermore there are signs that the climate of opinion is beginning to change. The permissive society has left us with a desperate crop of social problems. It was said that making contraceptives freely available to teenagers would reduce the number of unwanted pregnancies. In fact the reverse has happened and the abortion rate has soared. It was said that living together before marriage would produce more stable relationships. The opposite has resulted and now at least one marriage in three ends in divorce.

It was said that children would grow up to be more tolerant and accepting members of society if they were encouraged to choose their own standards of behaviour. But many young people in Britain today are suffering from a terrifying incidence of violence, alcoholism, drug abuse and general inability to cope with the pressures which face them. One social psychologist, attempting to explain this puzzling phenomenon, has suggested that we are at present experiencing a temporary upward bump in an overall downward trend in violent behaviour![2] It is not difficult to see that this is merely whistling in the dark. Incidents involving physical abuse of children have virtually doubled in ten years.

Such statistics give people good grounds for thinking that things are getting worse. At the same time our economic problems have drastically revised expectations of what can be achieved by the provisions of the welfare state. As a result many people today are disillusioned with the outcome of a privatized quest for happiness, have become aware that we must establish once again a strong ethical basis for society, and are conscious that a significant contribution will have to be made by individuals and voluntary associations committed to a caring role in a spirit of public service.

All of this is fertile soil for the Christian gospel. But we are bound to ask whether the churches are confident enough of their message and attractive enough in their fellowship to commend what they have to offer. Have they any right to expect that a spiritual revival in this country would necessarily flow in their direction? If there is a spiritual movement discernible in Britain today it is easier to see it in the peace movement or in commitment to humanity through gestures such as Live Aid than in any fresh discovery of the relevance of Christian preaching and church services. Nationwide evangelistic efforts such as Mission England may have helped numbers of individuals to find Christ, but there is as yet no sign of a general return to Christian belief. When there is a desire to seek Chris-

tian answers to contemporary problems these are often seen as
something different from the values the churches represent.

The 'pendulum' theory

The history of evangelical movements in this country over the
past 250 years has produced a pattern of alternating spiritual
decline and revival. As a result there is a tendency among
Christians to think that in due course the pendulum is bound
to swing back from godlessness to a fresh awakening. The
ravages of sin in society reach a pitch where people are driven
to seek God. On this basis the social predicaments of the
present age become the seed-bed for the Gospel and make
revival more rather than less likely.

   Such a theory fails to take account of a wider historical
perspective. Jesus may have declared that the gates of hell
would not prevail against his church, but this has not apparently
guaranteed the survival, let alone the revival, of the church in
particular places. Turkey is today a country with one of the
tiniest proportions of Christian nationals anywhere in the
world. Yet across its soil once moved the great apostle Paul
himself on his missionary journeys, planting churches in every
town so effectively that by the time the Roman Empire ceased
persecuting Christians at the beginning of the fourth century,
it is possible that the majority of the population in this area
was already Christian.[3] This was the stronghold of the church
in the early centuries.

   Again, it was the church in North Africa which produced
some of the most influential theologians and Christian leaders
in the West between the second and the fifth centuries. The
tiny church in those countries today is scarcely in a position to
offer any kind of intellectual leadership to the World Council
of Churches.

   Our Christian heritage in Britain is deeply rooted and the
witness of the churches does not seem to be about to vanish,
but there is certainly no kind of historical inevitability which
guarantees that future spiritual movements in this country will
necessarily be Christian. In John Wesley's time no genuinely
popular religious alternative to Christianity was available.
Today there are more Moslems than Methodists in Britain.
Loudspeakers broadcast the call to prayer from minarets.
Competition in evangelistic endeavour comes from many quar-

ters: Jehovah's Witnesses go round the housing estates; posters on the London underground advertise the blessings on offer from eastern gurus; television programmes explain the positive social usefulness of witchcraft; newspapers print the predictions of the wizards of astrology; Britain is now a market-place of alternative creeds. Even if these are not always promoted in an overtly competitive way the variety is nonetheless bewildering, as anyone who has visited the Festival of Body, Mind and Spirit will realize. Our pluralistic society encourages people to make personal religious choices, but the nation as a whole is no longer sure where its soul belongs.

Movements of renewal

Social conditions and historical processes thus offer no guarantee of revival for the churches: the only prospect for that lies within the churches themselves. Although it is true that reduced numbers may mean that churchgoers today are more committed to their faith, it is equally possible that loss of influence in society may have left the churches weak and demoralized in their mission. Hope of revival must therefore depend upon spiritual renewal taking place within the churches. A number of renewal movements have been evident for some time.

1. The Roman Catholic Church

A process of *aggiornamento* within the Roman Catholic Church was set in motion by the work of the Second Vatican Council, the opening message of which declared:

> We as pastors devote all our energies and thoughts to the renewal of ourselves and the flocks committed to us, so that there may radiate before all men the lovable features of Jesus Christ.[4]

Few could then have foreseen the changes in worship, lay involvement and ecumenical relations which would result from that Council.

Further signs of renewed spiritual life can be seen in a revived diaconate and in the basic Christian communities which have appeared in the Roman Catholic Church in Latin America and elsewhere. These will be considered in more detail later.

But renewal has not succeeded in changing this church's structures at many crucial points. For example, a celibate male priesthood is still insisted upon, despite totally insufficient numbers for adequate pastoral ministry. Also, the voice of the laity is still quite excluded from the making of important decisions.

2. *The ecumenical movement*
Jesus prayed, 'that they all may be one that the world may believe'. The importance of church unity for evangelistic work has given significant impetus to the ecumenical movement. In Britain official attempts to unite the churches have not produced impressive results since the war (the notable exception being the merger of the main body of Congregationalists and Presbyterians to form the United Reformed Church) but the development of co-operation and understanding between the denominations has been unquestionable and in some places a genuine local unity has resulted.

Despite some recent loss of momentum the great vision of 'one church renewed for mission' is still far more than a sad prospect of dying denominations clinging to one another in their weakness. Nevertheless there are warning signs that the renewing life of the Spirit today is often flowing outside the historic 'mainline' denominations which belong to the British Council of Churches. The ecumenical movement itself has sometimes been more concerned with structures than with renewal.

3. *The charismatic movement*
Another channel of renewal which since the sixties has affected all of the historic denominations to a greater or lesser extent is the charismatic movement. This has been effective in breaking down denominational barriers, with a unity centred in God and displayed in the work of the Holy Spirit overcoming obstacles created by man-made structures. Worship has become something to be enjoyed and a sense of expectancy that God is at work through Christians coming together has resulted in personal needs of forgiveness, healing, strength, deliverance and guidance being met in a public and sometimes dramatic manner in charismatic congregations. Moreover each worshipper is offered the opportunity to contribute in a distinctive

way to the life of his church through the exercise of spiritual gifts including prophecy and speaking in tongues.

Although this has created a bond more powerful than denominational differences it has also been divisive for those who do not share the charismatic experience. It has also in some cases created a rather superficial atmosphere of jollity and excitement. However, the effect on many congregations has been such that for them the word 'renewal' has come to be practically synonymous with the charismatic movement.

4. The rediscovery of the laity

One further aspect of renewal has been evident to some extent in all three of the movements already described, but is much deeper and more pervasive than any of them. It is the process by which increasing recognition has been given to the place of the laity in the government and ministry of the churches. Although this has in some churches always been recognized in theory, there is now some prospect of it becoming effective in practice, although the process is by no means complete.

The Church of England, for example, has moved from a period of clerical absolutism which lasted from 1868 until 1921 when Parochial Church Councils were established. These at first merely advised and co-operated with the incumbent but have now begun to acquire legal rights in deciding such previously clerical concerns as what forms of service should be used on Sundays for worship.[5] At the same time a form of national assembly including a house of laity has been developed and has now become the General Synod, with power to enact legislation recognized by Parliament.

The extent of change in this one church can be indicated by recalling that when in 1902 a committee was appointed to report on the position of the laity, it consisted of seven bishops, three deans, four archdeacons and six canons! More recently a similar task has been given to another group. This time membership consisted of six lay persons (including three women and one elder of the United Reformed Church) and four of the clergy. Their report, entitled *All Are Called*, notes that the New Testament teaching about the common calling of all Christian people has been rediscovered in the last thirty years by Christians of many different denominations:

We can thank God that it is now strongly affirmed by many members of the Church of England . . . (that) in many places 'the winter is past' and God's people have thawed out into active and fruitful service. They are responding eagerly to the call to be Christ's Body, and they are seeking to build up a common life together.[6]

The consequences of this 'unfreezing' of the gifts of the laity for the leadership and ministry of the churches will be the concern of this book.

As a result of such movements of renewal it is possible to point to many places today where the local church is far from dying; where congregations contain a good proportion of young people; where the worship is lively and participatory; where an articulate laity shares responsibility and works together to extend the mission of the church. At present the growth which is evident in such places barely keeps pace with decline elsewhere, but the experience of renewal is sufficient to encourage many to believe that a spiritually stronger church is gradually emerging and that eventually new life will spread through the church everywhere.

The problem of structures

Not everyone would share this hope. To some the imperviousness of the traditional structures of the churches to renewal is a far more obvious and depressing reality. Such people would acknowledge that the Holy Spirit has been known to work in spite of the structures, but that is to their way of thinking the whole nature of the problem. Who wants to belong to a church which has erected a series of barriers to the working of the Holy Spirit? Renewal by itself is not enough: renewal must lead to reformation in the church.

Without a readiness to reform the structures, the new life which is given in renewal becomes blocked and frustrated, preventing the church from becoming a channel of God's grace to the world. All too often the new life has been acceptable only if it fits itself into the existing structures. But this can seldom be more than a temporary state of affairs. If it is prolonged the survival of a church may well be in jeopardy.

The recent report of the Archbishop of Canterbury's Commission on Urban Priority Areas, entitled *Faith in the City*, noted some examples where renewal had resulted in changed lives and changed communities in some depressed parts of our big cities, but it was forced to add: 'Unless there is considerable reform this contribution will be progressively weakened, and in places the survival of the church itself may be threatened.'[7]

Reforming the structures

The realization that spiritual renewal in the church must lead to a reform of its structures is no new thing. Back in 1958 the Congregationalist minister Daniel Jenkins wrote: 'All churches need, as a condition of their renewal, a fresh realism in their assessment of how far their present structures enable them to fulfil their essential functions.'[8] He was writing from within the Protestant tradition, which has always in theory been committed to the principle of *ecclesia semper reformanda* (the church always in process of reform). In practice the Protestant tradition has been well nigh as rigid as the Catholic and Orthodox ones: that is to say, change has more often resulted in additional or alternative structures than in the satisfactory reform of existing ones.

In a local church it is always easier to start up a new organization than to close down or reform one which has outlived its usefulness, and the problem is greater when it concerns a whole denomination.

Additional structures

The process of creating additional structures, which is going on all the time, tends to produce confusion because the new is not always related clearly and constructively to the old. For example, a local church may introduce a new scheme for elders which is not clearly related to existing officers such as church-wardens or to the representative church council. Nevertheless the spontaneous growth of new structures is vital, to express the new life which is appearing.

In the late sixties an American Protestant scholar produced a list of additional structures which seemed to be required if the churches were to let the demands of mission influence their organizational pattern. These included:
– house churches;

- 'permanent availability structures', ranging from cathedrals to counselling centres and services like Samaritans;
- communities living together under a common discipline;
- 'task forces' concerned with particular projects;
- work-focused ministry concerned with people and structures in industry and commerce.[9]

It is interesting to note that since then attempts have been made to establish each of these approaches in this country, with varying degrees of success.

Unfortunately there comes a point at which the existing denominations have to consider how they absorb such developments into their systems. This can be a long, laborious and only partially successful process. The Church of England produced a Pastoral Measure in 1968 in order to give greater flexibility to the way in which it provided ministry through the parochial system. Its provisions included the formal establishment of team and group ministries. A revision of the Measure was completed in 1983 and it is already out of date in some respects. The Benefices Measure, first proposed to the General Synod in 1978 as a thoroughgoing reform of the system of appointing incumbents, finally took effect in 1986 having had all its teeth extracted.

Alternative structures

The time and energy required to carry through careful reforms of the existing structures with sufficient agreement in the older denominations can produce a frustrating sense that the churches are far too preoccupied with their own internal affairs. This is easily dismissed as a matter of rearranging the deck chairs on the *Titanic*. It is clear that reform has seldom if ever kept pace with the progress of renewal. One result has been that an increasing number of Christians have begun to despair of the historic churches and to turn elsewhere. For these people the established institutional and denominational structures are not the church. They may for a time have housed the church but they are now redundant and the real church, which is the pilgrim people of God, must once again move on.

Broadly speaking, among those who consider that it is now necessary to abandon the existing structures there are two views about the direction in which the church must move. One is toward what may be described as a network of basic communities and the other is to be found in the house church movement. Increasingly these are being seen as a way of replacing the present structures altogether in favour of simpler, and some would say more essential, styles of being the church. They express a quest for a renewed, youthful vigour in place of an institution riddled with arteriosclerosis.

Renewal through basic communities

Basic communities are Christian groups for fellowship, study, prayer and action working at grass-roots level in a manner analogous to the basic ecclesial communities of the Roman Catholic Church in Latin America and elsewhere. In their original context they are normally to be found among the poorest and most oppressed in places where the established church has not been able adequately to identify with their struggle through its traditional structures. Their primary focus is shared Bible study and prayer related directly to local social and political issues and to the experience of a particular community.

Although priests and members of religious orders often assist these groups by providing theological and other resources, the important thing about most of them is that their leaders are lay people from within their own community. Members generally remain committed to the Roman Catholic Church, but their vision of the church emphasizes collective responsibility and fellowship rather than an authoritarian and hierarchical model.

It is disputed how far this type of Christian group can be transferred directly to the British scene.[10] For one thing, there is no comparable popular working-class allegiance to organized Christianity in this country. However, the key idea is the power of the small group to achieve a deeper sense of commitment and fellowship and a greater freedom to engage in mission. Many examples of ways of seeing the essential unit of the church as the small group have become evident in this country in recent years, using a wide variety of methods. Many of these groups have been summarized by David Clark in his book *The Liberation of the Church*. They include experiments in communal living, in family support groups, in healing and prayer cells and networks, in attempts at a new lifestyle which is aware of the claims of the environment, in educational and welfare projects, in justice and peace movements, and in associations of disadvantaged and minority groups.

Such fellowship groups and voluntary associations have of course coexisted with the more formal structures of the church as a vital part of its life and outreach for many decades. Similar movements can be traced back to the religious societies of the seventeenth and eighteenth centuries, or even to the fraternities of the middle ages. What David Clark suggests is new is that Christians in Britain are beginning to find the centre of their spiritual life and witness in these communities rather than in the institutional structures. He writes: 'It is progressive, basic Christian groups (and networks) which I believe hold the key to the liberation of the church and to a new re-formation in the United Kingdom.'[11]

House groups and house churches

The house church movement also has roots in the rediscovery of the power of small groups, although the term no longer implies either a congregation of modest size or meetings which are confined to houses. The movement must now be distinguished from the house groups which have become a feature of many local churches since the war, the object of which has been to provide a more supportive fellowship and the opportunity for personal spiritual growth. Such house groups are conceived as entirely contained within and limited by the existing institutional structures. They are regarded by the clergy as principally a pastoral tool for building up the life of the larger congregation.

David Clark has noted that in relation to these house groups many clergy are 'either dominant and directive, or simply unco-operative, because they fear that such groups might become too independent and removed from the local congregation'[12]. In 1967 and again in 1986 the British Council of Churches succeeded in mounting courses to be followed in ecumenical house groups, but these remained very much under the control of the parent denominations and their local ministers.

Despite these restrictions house groups have clearly supplied, and in many cases continue to supply, an important ingredient in the renewal of the churches. The National Pastoral Congress of the Roman Catholic Church which met in Liverpool in 1980 produced a sector report which stated: 'We overwhelmingly recommend that parishes should become a communion of Christian communities incorporating small, neighbourhood, area and special interest groups.'[13] In similar vein the *Faith in the City* report recommends 'the development of centres, preferably ecumenical, in each neighbourhood (for example in house groups) which reach out in care and concern for the whole life of the neighbourhood and all its people. Small groups for prayer, Bible study, healing, and theological reflection on local issues would be based on them.'[14] It is clear that the established churches are going to continue to make use of house groups. However, they do not supply an alternative structure for renewal in the way that the separate house church fellowships have begun to do.

Renewal through house churches

When the charismatic movement began to spread through the churches house groups could often be used as convenient bases if the congregation as a whole or its clergy were opposed to too much explicit exercise of spiritual gifts in the Sunday worship. Sometimes this use of house groups had the active encouragement of a Minister who was sympathetic to the movement but had no wish to divide his congregation. It was perhaps inevitable that in time some of these groups moved away from their parent churches and produced their own leaders. Rejection by the congregation or frustration on the part of members of the charismatic house group led to a separate fellowship becoming established.

This is one way in which the house church movement has produced a number of separate fellowships in different localities which have now begun to develop networks and groupings across the country. These vary considerably in their teaching and lifestyle, despite a common charismatic emphasis. In particular, the authority of the leadership and the degree of centralization of the network are very differently understood and practised in different fellowships.

There are parallels here with the way in which the Christian Brethren developed in the last century. The Open Brethren are still distinguished by their strong adherence to the autonomy of each local fellowship, while the Exclusive Brethren have tried to keep each congregation in communion with all the rest by means of a central control which exerts autocratic power not only over each congregation but over each individual member[15]. Similar extremes are evident in the house churches.

The emergence of new denominational structures

The rapid growth of the house church movement is undeniable although in the nature of the case hard statistics are difficult to obtain. There may now be anything between 60,000 and 100,000 members of all the groupings put together[16]. Much of this growth, especially in the early stages, has come from disaffected members of other churches who saw no hope of revival coming through the unreformed structures of their own denominations. Up to a point, therefore, this movement can be understood as one expression of the basic Christian communities and networks which have already been described.

However, it now seems likely that a new denomination or denominations are in the process of emerging with their own parallel and alternative structures. The fellowships have not been concerned to remain small – far from it! In many places the description of 'house church' is misleading. Meetings of the whole fellowship may be held in schools, halls, or even in redundant church buildings purchased from other denominations. It is now common for house churches to be called Community Churches or Christian Fellowships. One section has become known as the Restoration Churches, this name indicating a distinctive position on church order. This teaching is not limited to those who are committed to membership of the so-called Restoration Churches.

Restoration teaching

The idea of Restoration finds a biblical basis in Acts 3:21, which indicates that after Pentecost the church is to look forward to a time when God will restore all things. Ultimately this can only be achieved by the return of Christ, but it is to be anticipated in the church by a restoration of the life of the New Testament community: 'Restoration means . . . doing the things they did at the beginning and being the kind of people that formed the Church.'[17]

The key to revival is thus seen as restoring the church as closely as possible to the New Testament model – to its pure, apostolic form. Whatever this means in practice, it will not spell the end of denominations, for it is largely the attempt to do just this which has produced the denominations. The Protestants of the sixteenth century, faced with the challenge of the Catholics to state where their church was before Luther, replied by appealing to the early church. George Fox in the seventeenth century wrote:

> Then I showed them that God was come to teach his people by his Spirit and to bring them off all their old ways, religions, churches, and worship . . . for they were out of the life and the Spirit that they (i.e. the apostles) were in that gave them forth.[18]

But George Fox is known today as the founder of the Quakers, not as the restorer of the primitive church.

This does not invalidate all the reformation movements which have taken place in former ages. There was indeed something normative about the principles which guided the life of the early Christian communities and to which later reformers have rightly appealed. Again and again this appeal has brought spiritual renewal into the life of the church as well as the less welcome consequences of controversy and division. But to attempt to produce a replica of the New Testament church would require certainty about two points: one is that we know what structure existed in those early years, and the other is that we are sure that it is normative for today.

In fact the evidence which the New Testament provides for the organization of the early Christian communities is incomplete and far from clear. Moreover, if it is remembered that the relevant documents were written at different times from different places it is evident that, as we might have expected, there was a great deal of variety as well as rapid change and development within the New Testament period[19]. To attempt to impose upon the biblical evidence the assumption that there existed from the first a uniform pattern only leads to the production of a new denomination. The foundations of episcopalian, presbyterian and congregationalist church government have all been read into the New Testament in this way. The historical assumptions behind Restoration teaching will in fact ensure the development of a rigid denominational structure with unusual speed. It is sad to see the mistakes of the past being repeated.

This book has been written in the conviction that there is a far more important way of appealing to biblical authority when it comes to altering the church's structures in response to renewal. Such an appeal should be made not to some supposedly normative structure for the church, but to the New Testament understanding of the nature of Christian community.

The gospel community

What, after all, was new and revolutionary about the community which Jesus founded? Allowing for the moment that he did indeed intend to found a community, how does that community relate to the preaching of Jesus concerning the kingdom of God? Much of the modern debate about these questions centres upon whether the church is meant to be an alternative society into which converts are baptized as a sign of separation from the world, or whether it is a sign of God's kingdom in the world and therefore not an alternative society but a model for human society everywhere. This is a distinction which has important implications for the church's mission, and the way in which it is answered will affect the degree of importance which is attached to existing structures.

But it is also relevant to consider the distinctiveness of the church, not from human society in general, but from all other religious societies. For whatever else the church may or may not be identified with, it is certainly understood to be the embodiment of the Christian religion. The case to be presented in the following chapters will be that the community founded by Jesus was based upon a radical rejection of the traditional basis of religious association.

Considered as a religion, therefore, Christianity is unique, and the community of believers must demonstrate that distinctiveness in the way in which they are organized. They are the gospel community: the community which proclaims the good news of Jesus. Only by understanding and applying that essential character to the problems of the contemporary churches will it be possible to see in which direction the structures need to be changed.

In order to bring out the radical nature of this gospel community with full emphasis it will be necessary first to look more closely at some of the features of the Christian religion as it manifests itself in Britain today through the organized churches. In the following chapters three aspects will be considered. First, *clericalism:* the dominant role of the clergy in the life of the church. Next, *cultic religion:* the way in which the churches provide for the religious needs, both public and private, of the citizens of this country. And finally, *institutionalism:* the preoccupation of the churches with maintaining their own existence.

It is the contrast between the state of affairs described in these chapters and the description of the gospel community which follows which gives point to the detailed consideration of changes in the local church which are set out later in the book.

2: Clericalism

'Be to us a father and a priest' (Judges 18:19)

First of all, the church is seen as the clergy. They possess a dominant role in the structure of the churches which can give them the power to obstruct what others may believe to be vitally necessary. Although there is a wide variety in the theoretical place and function which the different denominations accord to the ordained ministry, this has not made too much difference in practice to the influence and authority which the clergy exercise, both as a body within their denomination and as individuals in their own local churches.

Even among the independent Protestant churches, where congregations have the power to appoint and dismiss their ministers, the selection process is precisely to find a minister who will be able to bear the authority which the congregation intends to vest in him. R S Thomas, in his narrative poem, *The Minister*, describes how the deacons in a Welsh chapel

> *chose their pastors as they chose their horses –*
> *For hard work*

But once installed in that nonconformist pulpit, high above the people, the minister

> *wears the sober armour*
> *Of God, and wields the fiery tongue*
> *Of God, and listens to the voice*
> *Of God.*[1]

Catholic priest and Protestant pastor stand alike on holy ground. The churches of the Reformation may have been established as a reaction against priestcraft, but the sixteenth-century presbyterian Thomas Cartwright had a high doctrine of the ministry:

> God hath ordained the minister to this end, that, as in public meetings he only is the mouth of the Lord from him to the people, even so he ought to be only the mouth of the people from them unto the Lord.[2]

This was the standard reformed understanding of the role of the ordained ministry. The people still needed their mediators. Milton was not referring to the etymology alone when he wrote that 'new Presbyter is but old Priest writ large'.[3]

Apart from a few Christian bodies which have always been numerically very small, nearly all denominations are organized locally as a congregation gathered round a Minister. Clericalism is not the result of too much power being claimed by the clergy. It is the collusion of the whole church in an arrangement which makes the ministry of one part formative of the whole. The church is regarded as consisting of two unequal parts known as clergy and laity. The former, more important part contains the professionals in theological, pastoral and spiritual matters, while the latter contains the souls to be saved, the sheep to be fed, and the other ranks who wait to be led into action. The clergy line may be drawn in different places according to the denomination. Some churches have various types of non-commissioned officers supporting their officer class. But the structures of ministry in the different churches continue to reflect this clericalist attitude, despite the stirrings created by renewal movements.

In the Roman Catholic Church, as Schillebeeckx has shown, the Second Vatican Council did not basically affect the view of the laity as 'not-clergy', who stand in a subordinate hierarchical relationship to the orders of the sacred ministry[4]. The Church of England, despite modifications due to staffing shortages, continues to operate a nationwide parochial ministry dependent upon priests exercising the cure of souls. According to canon law each parish priest is the sole minister within his benefice. If there are other clergy they are licensed to him as 'assistant curates'. Under the Pastoral Measure a formal sharing of the cure of souls by a team of clergy has become possible, but if lay workers are part of the team they are not considered as having a share in the cure of souls. It is evident that the structures of ministry in the Church of England still keep it entirely at the discretion of the clergy whether there shall be any lay involvement in the ministry, and if so, what form it shall take.

Some other denominations have certainly included a much more significant role for their laity in their structures of ministry. The Methodist Church could hardly survive without its lay preachers who outnumber the ordained ministry by six to one. Nevertheless the authority which is given to the trained professionals remains quite obvious. Even in those cases where Christian groups have broken away from the established structures in recent years, as in the house churches, an authoritative leadership is often seen to be in control, and the authority invested in the leaders may even be heightened, as for example in the reappearance of the office of apostle.

The foundations of clericalism

Clericalism is clearly something which is not easily disposed of, however distorted may be the shape of a church which is infected by it. The reason for this is that it results from attempts by the churches to meet genuine theological and sociological needs which have to be provided for in one way or another. These may be described under four heads.

1. The need for authority

There is first the need to express the divine authority and commissioning of a church's ministry. Most forms of ordination reflect not only the church's choice of 'fit persons' to be pastors of the flock but also the authority of Christ himself as the Chief Shepherd who gives pastors to his church. Each ordinand is expected to have received a sense of inward call which is confirmed by what the Spirit says to the church. As a result the clergy seldom regard themselves as accountable simply to their congregations. They have a primary accountability to God who has called them and given them their ministry. This applies not only to those churches which have a sacramental view of ordination. The Protestant minister of the Word speaks with the authority of Holy Writ.

The climate of opinion today makes it expedient to play down this authority of the ordained ministry. There is much emphasis on the fact that Christ fulfilled his own ministry through the service of others, so authority is not to be exercised in an authoritarian manner. Consultation and consensus are now often held to be virtues in secular and in ecclesiastical government alike. But the readiness of some clergy to participate in a shared process of decision-making does not alter the fact that ordination implies recognition of divine provision for the church.

2. A focus of holiness
The sacred calling to divine office implies a consecration to holiness. The priest or pastor is a 'man of God'. This is not primarily a matter of high moral standards, although people naturally expect the church's ministers to set an example. It is about setting a person apart for the things of God. Human society has apparently not managed to exist for long without the appointment of priestly mediators who can handle the difficult episodes of birth, marriage, death, illness, warfare, natural disasters and so on, when people feel unable to cope with the problems of meaning and value which are raised. At such times there is a dependence upon the wisdom of the priest and the significance of the rites which he performs.

Christianity, like all other religions, is looked to as a source of such ultimate wisdom and significance. Even religions which have been founded in reaction to an existing priestcraft, whether Buddhism, Islam or Protestantism, have very soon produced their own revered holy men. So Christianity, even in those forms which avoid priestly terminology, seeks to provide for these dependent needs which inevitably become focused upon the ordained ministry which officiates at the critical moments[5].

It has been generally felt appropriate that this holiness or 'set-apartness' of the ordained ministry should be marked by observable differences in lifestyle, and this has sometimes produced difficulties of adjustment when people have been ordained to a non-stipendiary ministry and continued in their secular employment. Expectations of ministry from a representative figure in clerical dress have also limited what can be done to develop an 'every member' ministry in some local churches.

3. Professional competence
Most churches require those who are called to ordination also to receive training for their ministry. The content of the training has varied as the perception of the task has varied. From the

standpoint of the learned ministry of the Reformed churches, the medieval parish priest was often no more than an illiterate peasant who could just about read or recite from memory the necessary offices. Nevertheless his place in the community, his ability to use the sacred Latin tongue, and his access to the mysteries of religion in a society without books were quite sufficient for his ministrations to be accepted.

Today the relevance of a heavily academic and book-orientated training is itself being questioned. The emergence of other caring professions with their own standards of competence has led to a reassessment of the skills of the clergy. It has become easier to challenge their competence as teachers, counsellors, social workers and psychologists. There is considerable debate about what is the proper area of clergy competence. In popular estimation it may be knowledge of the Bible, skill in prayer, or even freedom from doubt. Among the clergy themselves some have fallen back upon a concept of 'general practitioner' ministering to the 'whole person', while others have concentrated upon what they see as the essential liturgical and sacramental functions. In both cases the requisite tool of their trade is theology, although this is itself a discipline which is in some disarray. In some churches management and personnel skills are given a high priority in what is expected from the clergy, while elsewhere the clergy react violently against such 'worldly' accomplishments, as if they might somehow get in the way of prayer.

The picture is undoubtedly a confusing one, but there is no doubt that the dominant position accorded to the clergy continues to depend in part upon the expectation that they should in some way provide a professional competence which the church needs.

4. The need for leadership

Even those Christian bodies like the Society of Friends and the Christian Brethren which do not practise ordination, have no professional ministry and expect all their members to be theologically articulate still have a need to recognize some form of leadership, whatever it may be called. It is doubtful if any human society can operate for long without leaders becoming more or less formally recognized, and where that happens there is always the possibility that the leaders will gain total control. The institutionalized leadership of the clergy which we find in all the major denominations has devalued the wisdom and experience of the laity. A newly appointed Minister will often be deferred to in a local church despite the fact that other church members have much longer experience of the local situation. Again and again where leadership is vested in a professional clergy the appointed leaders may not be the natural leaders.

It is often argued that the clergy enable change to happen, because without their contribution the local church would always be in danger of becoming static and inward looking. It is equally possible that the professionally trained clergy will arrive with a ready-made package of the latest ideas and once these have been applied no further change is sought or permitted until they move on. There is much to be said for local churches undertaking a regular process of review and redefinition of objectives, but many clergy are unwilling to engage in such a consultative process if it restricts their freedom to minister in the way they choose. Not many are yet ready to be involved in a regular appraisal and assessment of their own ministry. Clericalism has produced a leadership problem in many churches which is not resolved by the Minister occasionally allowing someone else to take the chair at council meetings.

Can the clergy promote reform?

The structure of the local church as a congregation gathered round a Minister provides a framework for meeting these basic needs for authority, holiness, competence and leadership in the church's ministry. But clericalism seems to be the inevitable result. Some would urge that renewal in the church could deliver it from clericalism without seriously altering the structure. A better trained clergy, clear in their vision of their vocation to enable the ministry of the whole people of God, able to share their authority and leadership without feeling threatened, can bring fresh life into the time-honoured structure. They can indeed, and in many places their efforts certainly assist in enabling the churches to move towards reformed structures. But this avoids rather than addresses certain inherent problems in the existing structures which can be focused by asking the following questions:

1. Why is divine authority and commissioning, as signified by

ordination, restricted to one kind (or at most three kinds) of vocation and ministry?

2. What does the common priesthood of the whole church mean if the structure directs people to focus their aspirations towards holiness upon just one Minister, or type of Minister?

3. How will congregations develop into maturity and accept responsibility for their own life and mission while they are dependent upon a professional ministry?

4. How will congregations grow beyond certain limits if their leadership is concentrated in the hands of one Minister who alone decides whether and how far to share it?

It is not surprising that much recent debate over the ministry has centred upon these or similar questions. New kinds of accredited lay ministry have been introduced in an attempt to validate a specifically lay vocation: there may be lay elders, lay pastors, lay preachers. This raises the question of what is signified by the perpetuation of the term 'lay', since such ministers have already been separated out from those members of the laity whose ministry is not accredited in the same way. The very existence of an accredited lay ministry may be seen as another symptom of clericalist attitudes in the church. In some cases, as often with Anglican Readers, the use of such ministries is explicitly to undertake clerical duties when no clergy are available.

The important agreed statements about ministry which have recently been produced by theologians of the major denominations take as their starting point that particular ministries must be related to the common priesthood which belongs to the whole church through its calling to share in Christ's mission.[6] However, what the Dutch Reformed scholar Hendrik Kraemer wrote about the priesthood of all believers almost thirty years ago in his book, *A Theology of the Laity*, remains true today: it 'rather fulfils the role of a flag than of an energizing principle'[7]. The churches continue to be organized into clergy and laity, the former being the ministry, the trained and normally paid professionals whom the laity support.

Often the attachment and loyalty of a congregation to their Minister will make the whole enterprise appear to be a system of maintaining and sustaining the clergy. Congregations which are dependent upon a professional ministry can become bereft and ailing if it is even temporarily removed. In rural areas when two or more Anglican parishes are to be put under a single priest the great issue is over where the incumbent will live.

Laity without clergy become sheep without a shepherd: they are still missionary-dependent, unable to attempt their own ministry. So generations of clergy ministering through the existing structures have not apparently managed to achieve anything resembling the grand objective of the apostle Paul: a whole church mature in Christ, in which each part is making its proper contribution to the welfare of the whole body (Eph 4:11–16). On the contrary, the chief desire of most congregations is to find someone as quickly as possible who can be to them 'a father and a priest'.

3: Cultic religion

'Our fathers worshipped on this mountain' (John 4:20)

Christianity has been the religion of the English peoples since their conversion to the faith beginning about a century and a half after they had arrived in this country. Our culture still has direct links with that of the Venerable Bede. Church buildings festoon the landscape wherever one goes in Britain. In the countryside it is quite possible to have three or four parish churches within view at once. The towns have churches or chapels on almost every street corner. Magnificent cathedrals adorn the centres of our historic cities. A visitor receives the impression that this is a religious country. It is perfectly easy for almost anyone to 'go to church' in the sense of visiting the building and large numbers of people in fact physically do so without engaging in a public act of worship while they are there. They are not all merely tourists. The use which is made of intercession boards and prayer candles indicates how many seek an opportunity for private business with God.

There are also specific occasions when a considerable number of people do still require the services of the church. People need cultic religion with its shrines and ritual to help them mark important milestones in life and invest them with proper significance: births, marriages, and especially deaths on the domestic level; coronations, state occasions, victory in war on a national level. Sometimes domestic occasions take on a wider significance to society, as for example funerals in the wake of a disaster or following sectarian killings in Northern Ireland. At such times people go to church *en masse* as an act of solidarity and to find meaning and hope.

Christianity as cultic religion

Some clergy refer to this use which is made of the priest, the building and the ritual as 'folk religion' and regard it as some kind of residual paganism. The fact is that Christianity has been providing the cultic religion of Western Europe for centuries. When people apply to the church for these purposes they are looking to the Christian faith to give significance to what they are doing. They are not necessarily using the church for their own superstitious reasons: they are availing themselves of what the structures of the church have historically provided to meet these cultic needs.

All of this continues to be true despite the steep decline in churchgoing during the present century. Apparently a smaller proportion of the population of this country today seems to think that it is important to go to church regularly on Sundays than at any time since the original conversion of the English. Surveys show however that large numbers of people profess to believe in God, and even in Jesus Christ as the Son of God, and claim that they pray regularly in private. To suggest that because they do not go to church they are not practising Christians would be received as a judgement not so much on their beliefs as on their behaviour. Churchgoing is suspect as a parading of one's religion and is widely assumed to be hypocritical. In popular parlance one can be 'just as good a Christian without going to church'.

Going to church and being the church

The essential element of Christianity which is lacking in this cultic religion is that of 'being the church'. This is a very different matter from 'going to church'. It will be demonstrated in a later chapter that the gospel community is essentially a 'way of being', and that Christ did not found a church for the purpose of ministering to cultic religious needs. But it ought to be understood at this point that those who want the benefits of cultic religion do not usually see the need to go to church regularly on Sundays. Unlike a national festival such as Christmas, an ordinary Sunday has no cultic significance in their lives. Cultic religion does not need a regular assembly of the faithful at all. There is no desire to 'be the church': that is something which is left in the hands of the 'religious' figures in society, such as monks and clergy. From this comes a powerful reinforcement of the attitude described in the last chapter that the church *is* the clergy.

Therefore the key question for the church when it finds itself expected to meet the cultic needs of a society is how it can do so and at the same time faithfully express the true nature of a gospel community. This is no new problem. Christians have lived with it since the time of Constantine. In a sense it has always been simpler for the church to be a persecuted minority than to play a recognized part in the life of the community. A particular difficulty lies in the fact that where Christianity has been thus 'established' for a long time the church inevitably becomes identified with the conservative elements in society. Consequently those who are concerned to undertake a prophetic ministry by pointing to injustice, corruption, discrimination and abuse of power on the part of those in authority frequently find themselves embarrassed by the cultic apparatus with which they are identified. Most prophets are compelled to call for reform in church as well as in state. On the whole the church has seldom been keen to consider giving up the status and privileges which long years of establishment have bestowed.

The opportunities of cultic religion

As with clericalism there are those who do not want to see the structures of cultic religion dismantled. They believe that the renewal of the church can come about through using them better. For some they provide important evangelistic opportunities by bringing large numbers of people into contact with the church's ministry. What they believe to be required is, firstly, careful preparation of the individual candidates, godparents, couples or families before the various rites are administered; secondly, clear communication of the Christian meaning in the rites; and thirdly, a good pastoral framework for support and follow-up. So baptisms are done within the context of the congregation's regular Sunday worship; Christian couples in the regular congregation assist with marriage preparation, attend the wedding and keep in touch; bereavement is seen as a time when people are often ready to respond to the offer of friendship which those who are 'being the church' can provide.

Others want to keep the traditional structures for quite

different reasons. They would challenge the assumption that the church is an association of those who have come together out of the community to be a fellowship of committed believers. This, they would urge, is the definition of a sect. The historic churches in Britain (pre-eminently the Church of England, but in practice today all the old and long-established denominations) are, whether they like it or not, the focus of the hopes and fears of the communities in which they are set. People want the church to be there, unchanging in a rapidly changing world.

The picture is not an even one of course: the churches have a much bigger influence on the life of the community in some parts of Britain than they can bring to bear elsewhere. Moreover it is quite possible that the position is now rapidly changing as the effects of an increasing pluralism work their way into the fabric of society. But for the present the churches still have this cultic role: it is what society actually expects of them and the consequences are liable to be serious if a local church is hijacked by an in-group who regard themselves as the committed faithful. If babies are refused baptism, or Christian burial is not provided for the departed, there is likely to be a fuss. As far as the Church of England is concerned the law still protects the rights of parishioners in these matters. It is therefore argued that the alienation from the church which results if such expectations are refused is wholly damaging to the Gospel.[1]

If the state were to decide to cease to give special recognition to Christianity and put the churches in the position of sects, that would be a different matter. But those who argue from this point of view would oppose the churches taking unilateral action to reject their cultic role, unless it could only be continued at the price of direct compromise with evil, as was the case in Hitler's Germany. For the present the churches continue to provide a Christian significance for the occasions and purposes of cultic religion.

Reform of cultic religion

It is further argued that the churches have the solution to the problems of cultic religion in their own hands, because they have every opportunity to carry through reforms of the rites and to educate the public in their reasons for doing so. In fact the outward forms of cultic religion have changed dramatically in recent years. Church buildings designed 'in the round' instead of on the traditional east-west axis, and the liturgical reordering of older buildings, emphasize the gathering together of the faithful rather than an invitation to man to attend the eternal mysteries.

The services, too, have been revised. The modern Anglican service for the baptism of children is explicitly for those whose parents are prepared to bring them up 'within the family of the church'; the congregation welcome the newly baptized into 'the Lord's Family'; there is a reference to 'the regular congregation'. All of this is intended to convey a sense of the importance of 'being the church'.

What is achieved by such reforms is more apparent than real. Often the message that comes across can still be one of 'going to church'. An immense amount of time has been taken up by many churches in recent years over revising the forms of worship. The Alternative Service Book of the Church of England is roughly twice the length of the Book of Common Prayer, and in 1986 another 300 pages were produced with services and prayers designed specially for the season of Lent and Easter. All of this has obviously increased greatly the material available for creating acts of worship.

It is taken for granted that meeting together for worship is essentially what is meant by 'being the church'. Many churches aim to have one main service of worship on a Sunday when the majority of the congregation come together. The basic activity of a congregation is a service. As a result, mission is easily conceived in terms of getting people to church. So the gospel community tries to live according to the basic premises of cultic religion, giving priority to the cultic acts, and the manner in which they are performed. It can easily be the gospel community rather than cultic religion which is changed by such reforms.

As for the large number of 'cultic religionists' in this country, the idea that modernising the liturgy will have the effect of getting more of them to church more regularly is far wide of the mark. What they want for their purposes is a sense of the traditional, the ancient and the mysterious when they engage in worship.

Cultic religion as a public service

As far as the cultic role of the churches in society is concerned, therefore, the result of these changes is a notable lack of communication. The words of the revised services are simply not heard to say what they are intended to mean. This is because the idea of church membership is completely inverted by the 'cultic religionist'. The model to which everything is related is the church established by law, namely, the Church of England. People in this country do not so much feel that they belong to the Church of England as that the C of E belongs to them. It exists to provide a public service. Membership is not just open to all: it is a birthright, whether use is made of it or not.

Other denominations do not escape the consequences of this, unless they practise very strict rules of membership. They tend to be regarded in their own neighbourhoods as privatized versions of the C of E, providing basically the same public service (and in fact a more useful one when it comes to the marriage of divorced persons).

What is this public service? At root, it is the affirmation of human activity through cultic ritual. The purpose of the ritual is not to change behaviour but to confirm that the behaviour is acceptable to God. For this purpose man has a natural need of priesthood and cult. Whatever form of ritual is used will make relatively little difference. The priest alone is expected to understand what the ritual means. For the worshipper, its significance is predetermined by the behaviour to which it relates. This accounts for the inability of many people to distinguish whether their child has been baptized or merely blessed. Similarly, the blessing of a marriage in church is easily made indistinguishable from the marriage service itself.

The significance that is placed upon the ritual will be a Christian one, although it will be Christianity defined in terms of behaviour rather than belonging, of doing rather than being. For example, when visiting the home of a deceased parishioner who has not been inside a church for fifty years the vicar will be expected to confirm the faith of the family that here was someone who never said a cross word and was always ready to do a good turn. In such a faith the rites of Christian burial will then be provided.

The future of cultic religion

It is difficult to predict how long the churches will be expected to go on providing the public service of cultic religion in a society which is increasingly pluralist in its beliefs. Prayers before council meetings in the town and county halls of the land are now widely regarded as a farce. When will a Christian coronation service come to be regarded in the same light? When will the majority follow the substantial minority who now look for personal significance to other faiths, or to the guidance of astrology?

Many kinds of priest are available today, ranging from psychiatrist-counsellors to technologist-witch doctors. The role of the Christian clergy as the natural priests of society is much reduced, and quite often mocked. However, the modern alternative priests of a secular kind have not yet developed any satisfactory last rites. The vast majority of the population still looks to Christianity for aid in the face of death.

The problem of cultic religion therefore remains for the churches. It traps them in a stance which is quite opposed to that of the one who said: 'Let the dead bury their own dead; but you go and proclaim the kingdom of God' (Lk 9:60).

4: Institutionalism

'What magnificent buildings!' (Mark 13:1)

The clergy and the 'cultic religionists' place considerable obstacles in the path of any reforms which are intended to allow the churches to exhibit more clearly the nature of the gospel community. But these obstacles are relatively minor in comparison with the sheer inertia of the churches as institutions, with their buildings, their bank accounts, their bureaucracies and their instinct for self-preservation.

Whatever power may be concentrated in the hands of the clergy, they do have to work in a voluntary association in which the laity constitute the overwhelming majority and are beginning to gain the right to be heard. In any case many of the clergy as individuals are anxious to encourage reform. This permits debate, even if it does not solve the problem of clericalism, which is a lay attitude as much as a professional one.

In the same way the assumptions lying behind cultic religion are increasingly being opened up for debate, not least because of increasing pluralism in society. It is now no longer so easy to assume that Britain is a Christian country. But every attempt to tackle the institutional problems of the churches seems to make the situation worse. Working parties produce reports, committees produce paper, but change is minimal.

As a result there are considerable numbers of believers today who fight shy of becoming involved in church membership. They identify with Simone Weil, who wrote: 'I love God, Christ and the Catholic faith . . . But I have not the slightest love for the Church . . . What frightens me is the Church as a social structure.'[1]

Such people are not to be confused with the absentee 'cultic religionists'. It is not that they do not see the point of going to church. They see only too clearly that the point of going to church is to be committed to an organization with a relentless round of committees, fundraising, rulemaking and in-talk. Individual Christians may take up their cross and be ready to lose their lives so that they might find them. Together as a church they behave as though survival is the top priority.

The image of the institutional church

The world is not deceived. The image which the churches project is one of any characteristic human organization with all the acquisitive and defensive attitudes necessary for survival in a competitive society. Church Councils spend many hours concerned with the successful maintenance of their buildings and activities. In how many of them is it taken for granted that the *first* claim on their resources of money, buildings and people is to meet the needs of others? More often such concerns are treated as the least important items in a church's budget, to be met only if anything is left at the end of the year when the fabric has been attended to, the church heated and furnished for the comfort of the worshippers, and the organ tuned to make a splendid sound to the glory of God. But for what other reason does the church exist if not to meet the needs of others? How else can it be a community which proclaims the gospel?

1. The wealth of the institution
So far from acknowledging that it has failed to spend its abundance on the poor the church casts itself upon public charity in order to preserve its inheritance. This paradox can only be explained by taking a particular example from the situation in which the Church of England is placed. Historically it has been one of the wealthiest institutions in this country. Like all the churches it possesses the tax advantages and the benefits of continuous administration which belong to charitable corporations. It therefore tends to conserve wealth much better than individuals who have to face death duties and shortage of heirs, or commercial companies who are subject to takeovers and in any case are not in the business of hoarding money.

Furthermore the church is subject to the terms of trusts and the requirements of the Charity Commissioners which make it much harder for it to get rid of its treasures. Generally speaking benefactors have wanted their capital to remain in existence so that their charity is not forgotten. So the church is laden with endowments, land, buildings, and treasures, all of which are very difficult to dispose of.

But having been acquired, all these things demand the spending of further money to keep them – to insure the buildings and the priceless works of art, to maintain the buildings, to administer the property and to manage the investments. The church's administration requires a civil service, much of it recruited specifically to carry out these maintenance tasks. Lawyers are needed to protect the church's interests as a property owner; architects, surveyors and other professionals must be employed to advise on means of preservation; members of the clergy who are admitted to office in the church are bound by oath to respect its rights and privileges.

It will of course be pointed out that the income from endowments is put to good use. It helps to sustain the living ministry of the church, and provides for those who have retired from its service. The spiritual advantages of this are doubtful, when some Church of England parishes now complain because inflation has made it necessary for them to find on average *almost half* of clergy stipends from live giving.

Moreover, considerable funds have to be devoted to conservation. It is always baffling to a tiny congregation which has given up the struggle to maintain its building and allowed it to become redundant, when the people then discover that funds are available to repair it after it has been closed. In Cambridge there is a redundant church which stands next to a theological college. It has not proved to be possible to allow it to be used by the college for training the living ministry, partly because of the objections of conservationists, but an enormous sum has been spent on its restoration as a museum piece[2]. Similar frustration occurs when virtually any treasure or item of church plate is put up for sale. There is a general outcry at such wanton dissipation of our national heritage even when what is being disposed of has neither been used nor seen within living memory!

These problems of inherited wealth are obviously more severe in the more ancient churches. But in principle there are few differences between the churches in the way they behave as institutions. Even the modern fellowships arising from the house church movement are acquiring buildings and bank accounts and in the process are building up reserves of earthly treasures with future maintenance problems. Some of these new churches are extremely demanding in the way they expect members to support the needs of the 'fellowship' (i.e. the emergent institution), for example by tithing. Would any of them refuse to take the fatal step down the primrose path of accepting legacies?

2. The maintenance of the institution

The Church of England, with its high profile as the keeper of many ancient buildings which symbolize the very history of whole communities, is inevitably in the business of maintenance on a grand scale. Architects produce reports on 15,000 churches every five years. This is designed to ensure that PCCs get on with essential repair work. The result is that huge sums have to be raised, often by small rural communities. Miracles have been achieved, with a bit of help recently from the state in specific cases, and for rather longer from interested trusts.

It is now true to say that our parish churches have never been so well maintained in any previous century. A recent survey commented: 'If the preservation of its church buildings is an indication of the strength of rural Anglicanism, the Church of England seems to be maintaining its position very well.'[3] But the same survey goes on to contrast this with the decline in the congregations and pastoral effectiveness of the church. Far from being burdened by the problems of maintenance the Church of England has made its tower restoration appeals and organ rebuilding funds into the very stuff of its religion of good works. Little else is discussed in some PCCs. A succession of church fetes and raffles are the yardstick by which progress is measured. The tragedy is not that money has to be spent on such maintenance work instead of on furthering the church's mission, but that the money could only be raised for such work. Without the restoration of the fabric the money would not be available at all, and one doubts whether some churches would be left with any mission at all.

The actual usefulness of the parish church is often strictly limited. A legal process known as obtaining a faculty is necessary before alterations can be carried out to any consecrated building. This will ensure among other things that the new work is normally done to the same expensive standard as the old. Since many congregations today want to install modern conveniences such as toilets, or ease of access for the disabled, or to adapt the building to make it less expensive to heat, to say nothing of installing kitchen facilities or reordering the furniture to make it more flexible for worship, it is not surprising that many faculties are needed (over 3,000 in 1982). Adapting historic buildings in such a way that they can actually assist the mission of the church can be a very costly business. And since their use is restricted to sacred purposes the number of hours on average that such a building is in use each week is in most cases very small.

The importance of the building is therefore more symbolic than functional, since on functional grounds alone there would be no case for retaining most of them. They would have been handed over to the state long ago as historic monuments. Yet parishioners struggle with might and main to preserve their churches. They are links with the past, shrines for cultic religion, separated spaces of holiness, signs of the sacred presence of God. They are not well suited to housing a gospel community.

3. The bureaucracy of the institution

Wealth and property are only part of the institutional problem of the churches. The administration of the larger denominations is becoming ever more centralized, but at the same time the process of decision-making becomes ever more consultative. The results include a burgeoning bureaucracy and formidable mountains of paper. In the Church of England since 1970 synodical government has developed a process of passing reports up and down the national, diocesan and deanery levels. The General Synod meets three times a year, for several days on each occasion. It bases its procedures on the secular model of parliament, with the familiar cry of 'Divide!' which is particularly appropriate, of course, when an issue such as church unity is being decided! The volume of business increases constantly so that despite watchful budgetary control the pressure is always there to enlarge the number of permanent committees, working parties and staff.

The ecumenical movement has also contributed to this process. While the British Council of Churches has its staff and committees, each member church also needs to maintain its own department for conducting its relations with the BCC and all the others. Issues of mission, social responsibility and so forth are often dealt with both ecumenically and denominationally, which duplicates effort.

The 'committee disease' also afflicts the local church. Clergy can find half their evenings taken up with meetings so that it becomes very difficult to make pastoral calls at times when people are at home. Active newcomers in a local church quickly find themselves co-opted on to bodies devoted to maintaining the life of the institution or its buildings. Meetings convened to discuss particular problems soon become permanent committees. People are organized round a task and find little time to meet each other in any depth.

Reforming the institution

A good case can be made out for believing that the church as an institution should find it no more difficult to reform itself than any other body. Progress has been made. Decisions are now made more carefully and responsibly; the administration is more accountable and efficient; stipends are distributed more evenly and better pensions are provided for the clergy; investments are morally as well as financially more judicious; buildings are in a better state of repair than ever before.

A constant stream of working party reports indicates the extent of the reforms which have been and are being made. Considered as an institution, any of the major denominations, from many points of view, has worthy features. The problem, however, is institutionalism – the constant tendency for commitment to and maintenance of the institution to become an end in itself.

Some structure is essential

And yet, what else can one expect? There must be some organization, some machinery of administration. Once it became clear that the church was going to exist for more than a short time an appropriate structure naturally developed. The mission itself was dependent upon it. Even in the New Testament period it is evident that collections were organized for the needy, ministry was maintained, administrative responsibilities were delegated, letters were written, contacts were kept up between different churches, councils were convened and policy decisions reached, and pastoral care was arranged for converts. Some of the specific ministries mentioned in the New Testament were administrative ones.

Commitment by some to servicing the organization has always been essential. History decrees that the burden grows heavier and the problems more intractable as the archives expand. The skeleton structure designed to service the needs of mission puts on weight and becomes instead a heavy load of precedent and procedure. As a result the church has to live with structures which have become so inflexible that they can no longer respond easily to new situations. Yesterday's new initiative becomes today's burden of maintenance.

Worse than that, the church's message to the world becomes distorted. How can such an institution convincingly proclaim that we are living in the last days, when all that is passing away must give place to the kingdom of God? A body that is so concerned with its own security and survival is unable to lift up its head and see its redemption drawing near (Lk. 21:28).

Inadequate solutions

One solution to the problem of institutionalism is offered by the house church movement. This proposes a mass exodus from the sinking ship of the institutional church. It is easy to see that the new lifeboat is itself going to run into problems in due course. But that may be to miss the point. The important thing according to this solution is to be free today to do what the Spirit requires. In the next century it may be necessary to leave the Restoration Churches for just the reason that the Pentecostals, the Christian Brethren, the Methodists, the Quakers, the Baptists and the Independents all found it necessary to leave the churches which were reformed in the sixteenth century. On this basis Protestant dissent becomes the life-principle of the church. Schism without heresy is the true path of renewal in every age.

There is a germ of truth here. Past movements of the Spirit have hardened into divided denominations because the existing institution proved incapable of responding to what God was doing. So today it is impossible to put all the blame on the breakaway groups. The ecumenical movement proceeds on the basis that all the member churches share in the life of the Body of Christ. Nevertheless the resulting state of disunity is at the very least confusing and, as the ecumenical movement itself testifies, many Christians have no doubt that it is in fact sinful in view of Christ's own prayer for unity and the harm which has been done to relationships between Christian groups.

But others would question whether it is necessary to allow separate structures to perpetuate such divisions. They believe that denominational differences can be transcended when Christians begin working together in a spirit of love. Unfortunately 'working together' only produces new structures. The most depressing thing about the ecumenical movement is the way it has preoccupied Christians with yet another set of committees, papers, conversations and bureaucracy, much of it at a very expensive international level. In fact we are probably past the stage when it was appropriate to speak of an ecumenical movement. What was an undoubted movement of the Spirit has now hardened into an institutional framework of ecumenism. The whole problem of institutionalism in the church is demonstrated by this one case. Meanwhile the Spirit's search for 'godly union and concord' in the hearts of believers goes on in other ways.

This survey of clericalism, cultic religion and institutionalism has highlighted the difficulties which are seen today by an increasing number of Christians to be impeding the renewal of the church. It raises urgently the questions of the nature of the church and its essential task. It is now time to consider what Jesus may have had in mind when he began it all.

Part two: The vision

5: The Gospel Community

The purpose of Jesus

Did Jesus intend to found a new religion? Certainly he did not set up a new religious organization with its clergy, cult and shrine. In itself this is not necessarily decisive, since the same has been true of other great religious figures: first came the Founder with his inspiration, and then the followers set up the organization. In the case of Jesus, however, his intention was clearly one of fulfilment rather than innovation. The same might be said in another sense of Mahomet, but Jesus stood within the central tradition of Judaism in a way that the Prophet could not.

Jesus was nurtured within a devout Jewish home. Luke's account of his early life repeatedly states that at the time of his birth everything was observed according to what the Law required (Lk 2:22–24,27,39), and that he grew up accustomed to attending the annual Passover festival in Jerusalem (Lk 2:41) and the synagogue each sabbath day in Nazareth (Lk 4:16). Although he attacked the observance of man-made traditions, Jesus neither attempted to reform the existing institutions nor summoned his followers to join a breakaway movement in the style of the Zealots or the Essenes.

His interpretation of the Law could lead him into some unorthodox behaviour: for example he was prepared to eat with tax collectors and sinners (Mt 9:10–13) and to ignore certain restrictions regarding the Sabbath (Mt 12:1–14). His quotation from Hosea ('I desire mercy, not sacrifice') in both of these incidents shows, however, that he could claim the support of the prophetic tradition in doing such things.

His moral teaching was certainly not in a liberalizing direction (see for example Mk 10:2–12), and he never for a moment encouraged his followers to neglect the Commandments, emphasizing instead the importance of observing them inwardly as well as externally and declaring that he had come not to destroy but to fulfil (Mt 5:17–48).

The ministry of Jesus was thus conducted within the religious framework of his own people. Although he claimed an authority greater than that of the religious leaders of his day, whom he criticized as 'blind guides', his instructions to those who came to him for help did not require them to act contrary to their familiar cultic practices (e.g. Mk 1:44; Mt 5:23f; Lk 17:14). Radical though his message was, Jesus was not apparently concerned to reform the institutional structures of Judaism.[1]

His cleansing of the Temple, recorded in all four Gospels, was not so much a reform as a prophetic act. He made other prophetic statements about the future of Israel's religion (e.g. Mt 21:43; 24:2). He stressed the primary importance of the spiritual relationship of the worshipper to God rather than the due observance of cultic ritual, but this too was directly in line with prophetic tradition (e.g. Mt 6:1–18; 23:23–28; Mk 7:1–23; Lk 18:9–14; Jn 4:21–24). Jesus was in fact called a prophet (Mt 21:11,46; Lk 7:16; 24:19; Jn 7:40).

But the kingdom of God which he announced was not to be equated with membership of a new organization, as the parables of the fishing net and of leaven, and of sowing and growth, all indicate. If his followers were undoubtedly from the beginning an indentifiable group, they also strikingly lacked all the distinctive features of a separate religious association.

Did Jesus and his followers then understand his mission as a renewal movement within Juadism? To this the answer must be both yes and no. He was widely accepted as a prophet, and some believed him to be the promised Messiah, or the Christ. For a brief period there was intense speculation over whether he would bring deliverance to Israel. But the deliverance which was looked for was conceived largely in political and institutional terms. Jesus did nothing to prevent the terrible disaster which overtook Judaism on these levels a few decades later. He offered no reform of the structures which would enable Judaism as an organized religion to survive in a hostile world.

Instead he summoned people to enter the kingdom of God, which was a hidden thing, like seed, like leaven, like salt. The object of his preaching was not to revive Judaism but to bring salvation. The salvation which he offered was the very opposite of survival, since it involved a willingness to lose one's life. It meant being ready to let go of all that was passing away in order to become part of the new creation which was the coming of God's kingdom. This was what it meant to be living in the 'last days'.

The early church

Jesus was disposed of by the Jewish leaders, but he left behind a group of followers who possessed two things. One was a belief that he had himself entered into the resurrection life which belonged to God's kingdom, and the other was an experience of the Spirit which communicated the living presence of Christ to the believers. On these foundations a unique community was established, a community which was expecting the kingdom announced by Jesus, a community which was experiencing the leadership of the Spirit.

1. A community expecting the kingdom

It has been argued that Jesus' lack of concern about providing his followers with an appropriate structure can be accounted for by his expectation that the end of the age was imminent. All that was necessary to prepare for this event, in terms of religious organization, was to appoint the Twelve to represent the tribes of Israel in the kingdom of God. On this view, the subsequent development of the church's organization became a legitimate, and indeed necessary, response once the end of the age had failed to arrive. But at what point could the early church conclude with safety that it *had* failed to occur? What authority has the church ever been given to stop expecting the *parousia*, the return of Christ? Jesus himself professed ignorance of the day and the hour (Mt 24:36).

Therefore instead of supposing that he had in mind a programme which would be fulfilled at an imminent moment, it is better to note that the arrival of the kingdom of God was the centre of Jesus' whole concern, so that he taught that all human behaviour should at all times be governed by anticipation of this event.

The coming of the kingdom, which was good news at the time when he preached, remains good news for us today. It depends no more today upon religious structures than it did in the early church. The church is indeed what C K Barrett has described as an 'eschatalogical monster', because it has had to exist for centuries as a body which is essentially 'provisional, temporary, penultimate'[2]. As soon as it begins to give an appearance of permanence in this world the church ceases to be a herald of the kingdom. For a successful perpetuation of its mission it actually requires a continual process of death and resurrection.

2. A community led by the Spirit

At the same time the church was a sign of God's age-long purpose in history. There was no break between the purpose of God to have a people through the calling of Abraham and the fulfilment of that purpose in Jesus Christ and his followers. The church was not 'founded' on the day of Pentecost, or by the call of Jesus to the Twelve. Jesus became in himself the appointed representative of God's ancient people, the promised Messiah. In him the chosen nation, the royal priesthood, could be rebuilt.

The Greek word for the church, *ekklesia*, had already been used by the translators of the Greek version of the Old Testament (the Septuagint) to refer to the congregation of Israel. They had deliberately chosen for this purpose a word which had no existing religious associations. Alan Richardson has commented, 'They well knew that the congregation of God's people was unique and that it could not be represented by any word which was used for a Greek religious society or pagan cultus'[3]. So in both Testaments 'the church' is regarded as a covenant community which is quite distinct from other forms of religious association.

In the Christian understanding, however, that community receives its focus in the life and ministry of one man, Jesus of Nazareth. Christ is 'not so much the Founder of the Church as he *is* himself the Church'[4]. It is only as his followers are incorporated into him that they receive a place in this community and a share in this ministry. This is the significance of the baptism of the Spirit (1 Cor 12:12f).

The crucial development which took place in this community following Pentecost is that it came to be understood that through the Spirit 'The Gentiles are heirs together with Israel, members together of one body, and sharers together in the promise in Christ Jesus' (Eph 3:6). There are plenty of indications in the Old Testament that this extension of the people of God was foreseen to be the destiny of Israel, as the New Testament writers frequently point out (e.g. Rom 15:8–12). However, the calling of Israel to be a priestly community bringing God's salvation to the Gentiles (Ex 19:5f; Isa 61:6) had not been realized, and in the post-exilic period the Jewish religion had become marked by cultic and institutional developments which emphasized the separateness of God's holy nation.

True holiness, however, was not a matter of cultic observance but of the bestowal of God's Spirit, as the prophets had already shown. The outpouring of the Spirit on the day of Pentecost was therefore recognized by Jesus' disciples as the fulfilment of the prophetic promise that in the 'last days' God would pour out his Spirit on *all people:*

> In the last days, God says,
> I will pour out my Spirit on all people.
> Your sons and daughters will prophesy,
> your young men will see visions,
> your old men will dream dreams.
> Even on my servants, both men and women,
> I will pour out my Spirit in those days
> (Joel 2:28f, quoted in Acts 2:17f)

So at last the true nature of the gospel community is realized. It is one in which all share in the ministry of the Spirit, all participate in the priesthood of Christ as ministers of the sanctuary, all have access to the Most Holy Place (1 Cor 12:4–11; 1 Pet 2:5,9; Heb 10:19–22). This is fundamental to the nature of the Christian Church. Unless its unique character is fully grasped it will be impossible to see that the apparatus of cultic religion, with its shrines and official priesthood, has no significance for Christianity, which, as a form of religious association, is not expressed by these means.

Humanity's religious quest so much demands the provision of a cult that it was not long before Christianity was equipped with equivalents of the Old Testament and pagan examples. Where the church has refused to meet these demands it has generally been misunderstood. It is commonly supposed that any living religion must achieve a harmonious co-operation between religious experience and its cultic expression. To assume that Christianity is like other religions in this respect, however, is to fail to see that for those who are 'in Christ' cultic religion has received a radically new interpretation. The language of cultic religion is not abandoned but deliberately applied in a wholly new way.

The Christian sacrifices, priesthood and temple

Although Jesus established no new religious system and his followers during the first century developed no cultic practices to match those which existed in contemporary Judaism and paganism, it is nevertheless a striking fact that the New Testament is full of cultic language, as the writers drew freely on the Old Testament imagery of sacrifice, priesthood and temple in their attempts to express their understanding of the gospel community. These terms were applied to Christ, as the one true sacrifice, priest and temple, and then to the church as being all these things in Christ.

1. The sacrifices

First of all, the salvation which Jesus had won for mankind was achieved by the shedding of his blood. In almost every book of the New Testament this is interpreted as a sacrificial act in language which reflects the Jewish sacrificial system[5]. But it is the letter to the Hebrews which develops this line of thought most extensively to show that the sacrifice of Christ is the one sufficient and effective offering which has made redundant all the ritual sacrifices of the Aaronic priesthood.

Does this then mean that neither the individual Christian nor the church corporately has any sacrifice to offer? On the contrary, the New Testament contains many references to the sacrifices which are offered by those who are 'in Christ'. Indeed, the whole community redeemed by Christ is referred to as a priestly community, that is to say it is composed entirely of priests who offer 'spiritual' sacrifices (1 Pet 2:5; cf Rev 1:5f).

The term 'spiritual' certainly does not exclude the material. Many Christian sacrifices referred to in the New Testament are very material indeed, such as the giving of money (Phil 4:18), hospitality and other gifts (Heb 13:16), and even the bloody sacrifice of martyrdom, the offering of one's life (2 Tim 4:6).

Paul bids the Christians at Rome to offer their bodies as 'living sacrifices' in a 'spiritual act of worship' (Rom 12:1). The significance of the word 'spiritual' is that such sacrifices are precisely not cultic ones. So the true Christian understanding of sacrifice is one in which the whole gospel community presents daily offerings of witness and obedience to the Lord through the Spirit. Not one of these is cultic, and there is no point in making cultic representations. Worship has to come right out of the sanctuary. The 'liturgy' of the New Testament church is something undertaken in everyday life.

So it runs directly contrary to this basis of Christian worship if the sacrament of the Lord's Supper is turned into a cultic act of sacrifice. Christians met together in each other's homes to break bread in communion with their risen Lord. The worship which Christians offer through their 'sacrifice of praise' (Heb 13:15) is at all times appropriately termed a thanksgiving, a 'eucharist'[6]. It is true that the Lord's Supper reminds us that no sacrifice can be 'spiritual' and acceptable to God unless it is the work of his gracious Spirit in lives redeemed at Calvary, but the result is not that the church offers Christ in the ritual of the sanctuary but that Christ offers the church to do God's will in the world.

2. *The priesthood*

The community which offers these sacrifices must be by definition a priestly one and reference has already been given to places in the New Testament which state this explicitly. Again the dissociation from a cultic priesthood is complete. Jesus himself was a lay person in Jewish terms. He had no right to enter the Holy Place and officiate on behalf of the people within the Temple of Jerusalem. But he claimed to mediate the grace of God more effectively than the cultic system:

> On the last and greatest day of the Feast, Jesus stood (in the Temple) and said in a loud voice, 'If anyone is thirsty, let him come to me and drink. Whoever believes in me, as the Scripture has said, streams of living water will flow from within him.' By this he meant the Spirit, whom those who believed in him were later to receive. (Jn 7:37–39).

At his death the curtain of the Temple which veiled the Most Holy Place was torn open. The letter to the Hebrews describes the ministry of Christ as that of a high priest who has not only himself entered the Most Holy Place to obtain eternal redemption for us, but has opened the way for all believers to enter the Most Holy Place by the blood of Jesus, there to minister as a sanctified priesthood before God (Heb 9:11–14; 10:19–22).

The outpouring of the Spirit at Pentecost created a priestly community which was able to worship God 'in spirit and in truth' as distinct from the temple worship in Jerusalem, the sacrifices of the Samaritans on Mount Gerizim, and all other cultic systems (Jn 4:21–24). Within this community there was no longer any separate order of priests. The New Testament never refers to any such group or office within the church. It is the entire community which is priestly. Neither is any special ministry needed to focus this priesthood. Each member is to offer, to 'present', their living sacrifices direct to God as their daily liturgy in the world.

3. The temple

With such a reinterpretation of priesthood and sacrifice it is obvious that the place of the Temple or sacred shrine was redefined as well. The documentary evidence suggests that this was the issue over which controversy between the followers of Jesus and the Jewish authorities was initially concentrated. Jesus prophesied the destruction of the Temple at Jerusalem and when he was arrested he was accused of plotting to destroy it (Mk 13:1f; 14:57f). A saying of Jesus was remembered that if the Temple were destroyed he would rebuild it in three days. John explains that he was referring to the temple of his body (Jn 2:19–22). Stephen, the first martyr, was also arrested for 'speaking against this holy place', and when put on trial he proceeded to preach a sermon on the theme that cultic religion always leads to idolatry, concluding with a reference to the futility of building a house for God (Acts 7:11–53; cf Paul in Acts 17:22–25).

This had much in common with the prophetic emphasis that God is everywhere present in his world: 'Heaven is my throne, and earth is my footstool. What kind of house will you build for me? says the Lord' (Isa 66:1f). This was something which cultic religion at its best could point to (e.g. 1 Kings 8:27–30). Again, the New Testament emphasis on participating through the Spirit in the worship of heaven, in the true temple which Christ has entered as our high priest (e.g. Col 3:1–4; Rev 1:9–18; Heb 9:23–26; 10:19–25) is something which is not incompatible with the use of an earthly shrine.

But beyond this there is in the New Testament an understanding of the gospel community as itself the temple. It is the people, not a building, within which God's Spirit dwells. The image of a building is central to the picture of the church (e.g. Mt 16:18; 1 Cor 3:16f; 6:19; Eph 2:20–22; 1 Pet 2:4–6). But it is a moveable building made up of 'living stones' in which God is worshipped everywhere through all the circumstances of everyday life. The idea of 'going to church' is quite foreign to the New Testament, whereas 'going to the temple to pray' is characteristic of cultic religion.

Christians made at first no distinction between service of God in the world and worship of God in a building. In fact service and worship are the same idea: it was in their daily work and witness that they offered their sacrifices. For example, Paul is able to speak of his evangelistic work using language taken straight out of the sanctuary: 'God gave me to be a minister (i.e. a 'liturgist', a word used of priests in the temple) of Christ Jesus to the Gentiles with the priestly duty of proclaiming the gospel of God, so that the Gentiles might become an offering acceptable to God, sanctified by the Holy Spirit' (Rom 15:16).

Given this terminology, it is quite consistent, although very surprising from our modern standpoint, that the meeting together of Christians is not thought of in the New Testament as being primarily to worship[7]. Of course when they met prayers were offered, and there is no question that the corporate dimension of worship is considered to be important. But teaching and fellowship are equally in view (Acts 2:42). The New Testament evidence suggests that the various activities which took place when the church met were secondary to the gathering itself, which was essentially for the purpose of awaiting the coming of the Lord, and thus proclaiming that they were in 'the last days' (Heb 10:25; 1 Cor 16:22; Phil 3:20; 4:4–7; Rev 22:20). From the first the breaking of bread in communion with the Lord was the action which articulated this longing of Christ's Body to be reunited with him in the coming of his kingdom (1 Cor 11:26).

The gospel community today

The true nature of the gospel community, according to the New Testament, is to be found in the faithfulness with which it expects the kingdom of God by living in the 'last days' as a provisional and temporary sign of Christ's coming; and secondly, in the way in which it is enabled by the Spirit to be a priestly community, offering acceptable sacrifices to God by its total way of life. Any structures for the organization of this community must therefore reflect its provisional nature. Any expression of its holiness must be profoundly 'lay' and 'worldly'.

Where shall we find this gospel community today? Everywhere the organized churches exhibit institutional permanence and maintain shrines and sacred ministries for the performance of cultic ritual. Temple, priest and sacrifice in their cultic sense once again dominate the life of the gospel community. Throughout history groups have broken away from the established churches in an attempt to recover something of the 'provisional, temporary and penultimate' character of a body which is living in the 'last days'. But the inevitable necessity of having *some* degree of organization, the powerful temptation to seek self-preservation, and the basic human desire to separate off what is sacred from what is 'worldly' have always proved too powerful and in due course another cultic system has resulted. To put it bluntly, the gospel community is unsuitable for fulfilling the religious needs of mankind, which continue to demand the provision of shrines and cultic priesthoods.

But is it right to judge the gospel community by religious criteria which are implicitly assumed to apply to a limited area of human experience, albeit an area which is intended to focus the whole? In Christ mankind has been offered not a new religion, but a new life. Predictably, mankind has responded by attempting to reduce the gospel to a new religious system.

However, the gospel community is made up of those who know what Paul meant when he wrote that 'if anyone is in Christ, he is a new creation' (2 Cor 5:17). That 'new creation', which is the firstfruits of the kingdom, has to be lived out within the old world order if the kingdom is to appear. That includes the old religious order. Here Christ is the model who, as has been shown, fulfilled his own ministry within the existing religious framework of his day.

Returning therefore to the questions which were considered in the first chapter, as to whether it is possible to reform the existing church structures, or whether new ones must be created if revival is to come, it is now evident that both questions are misconceived. Christ himself sought to do neither. He sought to bring salvation by preaching the good news of the kingdom, which is a hidden thing. And always in the organized churches, where the gospel is being preached, the Spirit is doing a hidden work which may from time to time and in different ways become evident in the structures, but must not be confused with structural reform.

The gospel community relates to church structures as a new building to the scaffolding which surrounds it. Reforming the structures is like reorganizing the scaffolding: it may be necessary but it does not in itself alter the actual building at all. Creating alternative new structures is like replacing the scaffolding: it may be useful, but then again it may be a waste of time.

Down the ages the Spirit and the Word of God have continued to create the gospel community. It is not an invisible body: it does require some structure to grow and express itself. During times of persecution it may have to go underground; at other times its actual expression may be highly visible, taking any of a wide variety of cultural forms, all of which will be imperfect. Through them all there must be a proclamation of the good news, and the good news is not the church but the kingdom, the reign of Christ over every area of life.

6: Leadership in the Gospel Community

The gospel community was described in the last chapter as something radically different from the cultic systems of the world's religions. Although Christianity has itself long since provided a further such system (or rather numerous systems) to meet man's religious requirements it was in origin a missionary movement proclaiming the kingdom of God over the whole of creation through its Saviour Jesus Christ. For this purpose it reinterpreted the cultic apparatus of priesthood, sacrifice and temple in terms which included the whole Christian body and thus completely abolished the ancient distinctions between priest and people, sacred and profane.

Historically the church has sustained its mission by assuming many forms in different cultural contexts. Different patterns of leadership have developed. It is a mistake to assume that those forms which have the greatest antiquity have the most authority; or conversely that what is operative today is fixed. All outward forms of Christianity are constantly changing, and none can claim Christ's authority since his concern was with the gospel community itself and not with any particular institutional form of it.

Authority for ministry

This assertion would certainly be challenged by those for whom the church's authority is inseparable from its institutional form. They would claim that while Jesus may not have set up a religious organization he did commit his juridical and pastoral authority to the Twelve, who in turn had the power to pass it on to their successors. In other words the claim is that Jesus did give to the original community a Spirit-filled leadership which eventually, through an apostolical succession of ministerial authority handed down to each succeeding generation, became responsible for the highly structured institution which in time developed. Thus it is possible, in this derivative sense, to claim Christ's authority for the clergy, the canon law, the liturgies and the consecration of sacred buildings. What evidence is there for this view?

1. Christ's commission

There are certain passages in the New Testament which suggest that the early church was conscious of having received authority from Christ for its leadership. For example, in Matthew 16:13–20 Jesus describes Simon Peter as the rock on which he will build his church (one of only two references to 'church' in the Gospels), and states that he will be given 'the keys of the kingdom of heaven' with the power of 'binding' and 'loosing'. Again, in John 20:19–23 the risen Christ shows himself to his disciples and commissions them to go in his name (cf. Mt 28:19; Mk 3:14); then he breathes on them and says: 'Receive the Holy Spirit. If you forgive anyone his sins, they are forgiven; if you do not forgive them, they are not forgiven' (cf Mt 18:18). At the beginning of the book of Acts Jesus instructs the apostles 'he had chosen' to wait in Jerusalem for the baptism of the Holy Spirit which would empower them to be his witnesses 'in Jerusalem, and in all Judea and Samaria, and to the ends of the earth' (Acts 1:1–8).

It is not surprising that such crucial passages have become the focus of a great deal of scholarly attention and varying interpretation. Perhaps the key question is how inclusive the authority given by Christ is intended to be. In Matthew's gospel it is Simon Peter alone who is given authority in chapter 16, at which point he alone had confessed his belief in Jesus as the Christ. All the disciples are included, however, in a similar commissioning in chapter 18. In John's gospel it is 'the disciples' who are addressed. This may mean the Twelve, although it is certainly capable of being understood as the whole company of believers (cf Jn 20:24; 6:66–71).

The reference in Acts is explicitly to the chosen apostles, and the number of twelve is made up by the election of Matthias by lot to replace Judas. Nevertheless the fulfilment of the commission to be witnesses 'to the ends of the earth' evidently involved all the believers. Indeed, it is specifically recorded in

Acts chapter 8 that the gospel came to Samaria because the believers 'except the apostles' were scattered following the death of Stephen, and 'those who had been scattered preached the word wherever they went' (Acts 8:1–5). There is no consistency about the use of the title 'apostle' either, since it is applied several times in the New Testament, including the book of Acts (e.g. 14:4), to Christian leaders who were not among the Twelve, Paul being the most notable but by no means the only example.

2. Apostolic authority

When these points are taken into consideration it is possible to conclude that the commission to preach the gospel was given by Christ to the whole Christian community. The Twelve were chosen in the first place not to be the leaders so much as the nucleus of that community. The number is twelve because that symbolizes the whole people of God. On the day of Pentecost they stood up as the foundation members to which 3,000 converts were added (Acts 2:41f); other believers already existed (Acts 1:15), but the Twelve were the chosen witnesses to the resurrection (Acts 1:22). This part of their role admitted of no successors and is perpetuated in the New Testament writings.

But the apostolic task of founding new churches was soon shared with others. As the mission progressed the position of most of the Twelve seems, from the evidence of the New Testament, to have become fairly obscure[1]. Of course, we do not possess a fully documented history, but it is clear from Acts chapter 15 that even at Jerusalem a group of elders had emerged to share leadership with the apostles. No doubt while they lived the Twelve (and some others) continued to possess the authority of those who had seen and heard Jesus: 'That which was from the beginning, which we have heard, which we have seen with our eyes, which we have looked at and our hands have touched – this we proclaim' (1 Jn 1:1).

But the historical evidence does not support a picture of them ruling over the growing churches. Neither the Twelve, nor Paul, nor anyone else who shared in the apostolic ministry possessed any kind of universal jurisdiction. As James Dunn has demonstrated, 'The apostle exercised authority within a community not as an "apostle of the universal Church", but as the founder of that community; his authority as apostle in a church sprang from his work in bringing that church to birth.'[2]

3. Leadership in the early church

Among the New Testament writings, which of course cover a period of rapid change and development, it is possible to discern some churches which looked to the immediate and direct guidance of the Holy Spirit, some which continued to be dependent upon travelling apostles, prophets and evangelists, and some which had developed their own pattern of local oversight. In one of the earliest New Testament documents, Paul's first letter to the Thessalonians, there is a reference to workers who lead and guide the church (1 Thess 5:12) but no titles are mentioned. Later on overseers (*episkopoi*) and deacons appear (Phil 1:1). The book of Acts gives a picture of elders (*presbyteroi*) being appointed in the congregations founded by Paul and his companions and a similar group appears at Jerusalem (Acts 14:23; 15:2; 21:18). Elders and overseers (presbyters and bishops) were probably alternative names for the same or equivalent leaders in these local churches (cf Acts 20:18,28).

There is no clue in the New Testament as to why these titles came to indicate separate offices later on. Elders may literally have been the older men at first, or at any rate the seniors among the early converts who were thus likely to be more mature and able to accept responsibility for the nurture of those who were newly born in the faith. By the time that the Pastoral Epistles were written there was, in some of the Pauline congregations at least, a much greater concern with the twofold 'official' leadership of overseers/elders and deacons. A similar concern was no doubt felt in many places following the deaths of the apostles and their companions. There was also the threat of false prophets and apostles. The Pastorals and the letters of John reflect the need to protect the flock by the formal appointment of leaders.

Where did the authority of this emergent local leadership come from? Not from the Twelve. As a recent report has admitted, 'The New Testament contains no explicit record of a transmission of Peter's leadership; nor is the transmission of apostolic authority in general very clear.'[3] It is not clear because it did not exist. Nor is there much evidence of the apostolic founders of local churches giving guidance on the transmission of authority. The account in Acts, for example, of Paul bidding farewell to the Ephesian church leaders is no help on the subject of how the elders are to provide for their succession. Despite his warnings about danger from 'savage wolves' who 'will not spare the flock', he lays down no code of practice: instead he commits them 'to God and to the word of his grace' (Acts 20:17–38).

To take another example, Paul writing to the Corinthians is positively casual compared to Clement writing to the Corinthians a few decades later. Clement is very concerned with securing church order through a due succession of ministry. Paul mentions no orders of ministry at all. Certainly he is concerned with the need to discipline those who bring the fellowship into disrepute, and to ensure that the exercise of gifts within the congregation is done in a worthy and edifying manner. But in all this he is merely stating general principles and pointing to examples he knows of where they have been neglected at Corinth. He himself makes no attempt to impose an organization, nor does he appeal to those who are the leaders to exercise their authority. His remarks are addressed to all the brothers, the whole church at Corinth. His only reference to ministerial appointment is to those who, like Stephanas, had 'appointed themselves' to the ministry of serving the needs of others (1 Cor 16:15).

This evidence suggests that in at least some of the Pauline churches authority was shared by the whole body, because the whole body shared in the charismatic ministry of the Spirit. In his study, *Jesus and the Spirit*, James Dunn has concluded that 'authority in the primitive church was primarily charismatic in nature'[4]. That does not necessarily mean a kind of democratic free-for-all, because it was possible for the community to recognize that the gifts of the Spirit included ones which were appropriate for leadership. The existence of leadership gifts is explicitly described in Ephesians 4:7–16, for example, as being necessary to mobilize the ministry of the whole body, so that 'each part does its work'. These leadership gifts are specifically stated to be bestowed by the ascended Christ. Authority in the church is not regarded as something transmitted through a historical succession of leaders, but as the direct provision of Christ to the church in every age.

Moreover the leadership ministries which are listed in this passage are not the 'official' ones of bishops, presbyters and deacons. The important thing is not to fill vacant offices but to recognize the gifts for leadership of apostles, prophets, evangelists, pastors and teachers. Such are Christ's charismatic provision of leadership for building up the church. So authority for ministry is given by Christ to the whole church, which recognizes the particular gifts which have been bestowed upon each individual, including those who are to be appointed to any leadership function. One recent writer has spelt out the implications for those who today persist in seeing authority in the church in terms of status: 'It is a complete misreading of the New Testament which assumes that those appointed elders have an authority inherent in their office.'[5]

Corporate leadership

The existence of a number of different leadership gifts corresponds to the fact that there are a variety of leadership functions necessary within the church. It is therefore not surprising that the evidence of the New Testament suggests that from the beginning a corporate leadership was the norm. Nowhere do we discern anyone who might be described in modern parlance as 'the Minister' of a local church. For example, the leadership at Antioch in Acts 13:1 consisted of a group of 'prophets and teachers'. From among these two, Barnabas and Saul, are commissioned to go on a missionary tour.

On all his journeys thereafter Paul was inseparable from a group of missionary companions. He considered that he was greatly impoverished if he was reduced to but a single fellow worker (2 Tim 4:11; cf the picture of team ministry conveyed by Col 4:7–15). All the references to the appointment of elders (presbyters) as leaders of local churches indicate a group or college of them. There is no mention of a single leader. In fact, one who 'loves to be first' is rebuked (3 John 9).

This pattern of corporate leadership is not just a safeguard against dominant characters. It is part and parcel of understanding the leadership of the Holy Spirit through a diversity of gifts. The second-century development of a single bishop as a focus of unity was no doubt prompted by problems with splinter groups, but it was still seen as a ministry exercised within and as part of a corporate presbyterate. So central is this corporate leadership to the life of the early Christian communities that it is astonishing that the pattern of leadership in the churches today should be so far removed from it, even in principle.

The important theological document of the World Council of Churches on *Baptism, Eucharist and Ministry* achieves a masterpiece of understatement when it observes that 'in some churches the collegial dimension of leadership . . . has suffered diminution'[6]. The fact is that in all major denominations it has been almost totally lost to sight. The inherited tradition is of a single leader to each congregation. This is so taken for granted that many seem to assume nothing else could work, and therefore if the early church had a different pattern it must have been found to fail.

Is this true? James Dunn considers the possibility that 'the Pauline vision of charismatic community . . . is unworkable in practice' because it is so vulnerable to the weaknesses of individual members; but he notes that 'the alternatives suffer from even graver weaknesses and are exposed to more serious dangers', as history has abundantly shown[7]. An important change occurred in the second century when bishops came increasingly to exercise oversight of more than one local church. A consequence of this was that the college of presbyters became individually responsible for presiding over separate congregations, since the bishop could not be in all places at once. This entailed a fragmentation of the corporate leadership and the identification of individual presbyters with particular congregations. Units of pastoral care were established.

Today, episcopal churches retain the theory of a college of presbyters in each diocese, but this is very far removed from shared leadership in a local church, especially in those places where each diocese contains hundreds of parishes. In any case, the cure of souls in each parish is allotted to an individual except where a modern team ministry has been set up.

The Reformed churches of the sixteenth century went back to scripture and reintroduced a corporate eldership in the local church. However, the high standard of preaching and pastoral work which has been such an admirable feature of the full-time 'professional' ministry in these churches has undoubtedly set the teaching elders on a higher plane of authority which has often obscured the shared responsibility of the local oversight. In any case, the norm has been to appoint and pay one teaching elder to be 'the minister'. Even those churches which have embraced a congregational form of church order have often in practice been ready to leave the pastoring to the paid Minister, on the principle that you do not hire a dog and bark yourself.

Priesthood

Over and above the human weaknesses and the organizational changes which may have led to the loss of emphasis on shared leadership in the church, there was also another even more powerful factor at work, reasserting the priorities of cultic religion within the early Christian missionary movement. In the New Testament the word for 'priest' (*hiereus*) is never applied to a particular office within the church. It is a term which is equally applicable to all the members of the body of Christ. No differentiation or hierarchy exists in the terminology which is used in the early church for the priestly calling and ministry of all Christian people. By the end of the fourth century a very different state of affairs existed. A theologian like John Chrysostom could write a work *On the Priesthood* in which *hiereus* is used instead of *presbyteros* to refer to the ordained ministry, and the great reality of this ministry is its sacred cultic work within the shrine:

> The office of priesthood is performed on earth, but it ranks among heavenly things . . . When you see the Lord offered there in sacrifice, and the priest standing and praying, and all being reddened by the precious blood, do you feel that you are still standing among men, on earth? . . . For the priest as he stands there brings down . . . the Holy Spirit . . . You will easily realize to what dignity the grace of the Holy Spirit has raised priests . . . They have received a power which God did not give to angels or archangels . . . for what priests do on earth God confirms on high . . . What is given to them is nothing less than a heavenly authority . . . "The Father has entrusted all judgement to the Son": and here I see the Son giving it all into the hands of his priests.[8]

The message of Jesus which created a gospel community by its radical reinterpretation of the meaning of priesthood, sacrifice and temple has here become lost once more in a smokescreen of 'holy' worship.

Modern ecumenical documents generally recognize that there is no biblical basis for using the terms 'priest' or 'priesthood' as an exclusive description of the church's leadership, but nevertheless accept them as applicable in a limited sense. For example the WCC statement on *Baptism, Eucharist and Ministry* says: 'When the terms are used in connection with the ordained ministry, their meaning differs in appropriate ways from the sacrificial priesthood of the Old Testament, from the unique redemptive priesthood of Christ and from the corporate priesthood of the people of God.'[9] The difference in meaning, however, is not defined.

The ARCIC *Final Report* says in the statement on 'Ministry and Ordination': '(Ordained) ministry is not an extension of the common Christian priesthood but belongs to another realm of the gifts of the Spirit.'[10] This is explained in the subsequent 'Elucidations' as follows:

> The ordained ministry is called priestly principally because it has a particular sacramental relationship with Christ as High Priest . . . It is only the ordained Minister who presides at the eucharist, in which, in the name of Christ and on behalf of his Church, he recites the narrative of the institution of the Last Supper, and invokes the Holy Spirit upon the gifts. The word *priesthood* is used by way of analogy when it is applied to the people of God and to the ordained ministry. These are two distinct realities which relate, each in its own way, to the high priesthood of Christ, the unique priesthood of the new covenant, which is their source and model.[11]

Experience has shown, however, that the priestly role of the clergy has extended far beyond the limited function described here of representing Christ to the congregation in the eucharist, central though that has been. It is doubtful if any clergy who understand their ministry in sacerdotal terms would be happy with such a restricted definition. From the representative sacramental role is derived an authority which extends to every part of their ministry. This has powerfully reinforced the dependence of the congregation upon a single (priestly) minister and made it much more difficult to recover a biblical emphasis upon shared leadership. It would seem therefore that the limited usefulness of applying priestly terminology to church leaders is far outweighed by its disadvantages in heightening clericalism and in obscuring the true nature of the gospel community. Because it is not used at all in the New Testament in this way there is no ground for asserting that there is anything obligatory about it, and since it is at best ambiguous it is better dropped. The term 'priest' ought to be replaced by 'presbyter' or 'elder' wherever it is in use in the church to describe a particular order of ministry.

Ordination

The leadership ministries of apostles, prophets, evangelists, pastors and teachers require corporate expression and recognition within a leadership team in each local church. However, the various titles which occur in the New Testament to describe the emerging 'official' leadership (bishops/overseers, presbyters/elders, and deacons), which have historically been marked out by ordination, significantly do not indicate particular leadership gifts. There has never been any systematic attempt to recognize each gift by the creation of a separate order of ministry. This shows that ordained or 'official' ministry exists to serve a broader spiritual purpose in a church where a multiplicity of gifts are being exercised by the total membership. If today there were greater recognition that ministry is the responsibility of the whole laity this broader purpose for the ordained ministry would more clearly be seen. It may be summarized under three heads.

1. The provision of 'oversight'
The more active a church may be in developing an 'every member' ministry involving the gifts of all the members, the greater will be the need for what the New Testament calls 'oversight' (*episkope*). Individual members have to fulfil their particular ministry, but there must be some who are concerned with the welfare of the whole body. Such an 'oversight' ministry is needed at various levels. There will be those who undertake the apostolic work of the 'care of all the churches'; there will be a group of elders sharing responsibility for the 'oversight' of a local church; wherever a group of Christians meet in house churches or small rural communities pastoral provision for them as a group is essential.

2. A focus of unity
In the face of counterfeit ministries and false gospels the New Testament writers clearly saw the need to keep the churches

true to apostolic teaching. Their writings continue to serve that essential purpose. But the way in which the life of the churches is ordered ought to express this unity in the faith. This is what is generally understood by intercommunion and it is not surprising that recognition of each other's ordained ministries is so often the test of this unity. Sadly, the grounds on which communion is broken are often the secondary ones of the institutional form of such ordained ministry. *Baptism, Eucharist and Ministry* has expressed a timely warning on this: 'The churches . . . need to avoid attributing their particular forms of ordained ministry directly to the will and institution of Jesus Christ.'[12] This is because Christ has given the gospel community no authoritative institutional form. Had he done so, it would no longer be a community exhibiting the provisional and temporary existence of the 'last days'.

Certainly the ordained ministry is in no way sustained by a historical continuity, but by the charismatic gifts of the ascended Christ today. Nevertheless recognition of some at least of the local church's leadership by the wider church is important. A form of ordination which associates the leadership ministry locally with that which is recognized elsewhere can give a focus of unity and intercommunion. Those who preside in the local assembly should be leaders whose ministry is thus recognized. In this way the local church expresses the truth that those who break the one bread are indeed one body: one, that is, with the church everywhere.

3. A representative authority
A further development of the two previous points places in the ordained ministry an authority which can speak and act on behalf of the whole body, both at local and wider level. There is a vital role for 'linking' ministries which maintain contacts between the churches, broaden horizons and bring fresh vision to those whose ministry is confined to a single place, and extend the apostolic and missionary task of the gospel community where it could not otherwise be attempted. In his study of the early development of the church's ministry Max Thurian has described this process in the following way:

  While the ministries in the local church were being organized into a college of elders with a leader, the ministry of the apostles and their helpers was continuing and ensuring a link between all the churches. This universal apostolic ministry still remained valid and necessary so that the local churches did not lose contact.[13]

On the basis of the threefold purpose just outlined it can be argued that a recognized and ordered leadership ministry is needed by the church. It will be composed of individuals whom the church considers to have been called by Christ and equipped with the appropriate leadership gifts. Since the rest of this book will be concerned principally with how to develop and sustain an effective corporate leadership *within* the local church, it is important to affirm here the necessity of that local 'oversight' being related, through the ordination of some of its members at least, to the recognized leadership of the churches elsewhere. In other words, a local ordained ministry should be seen as an important component part of the leadership team in each church.

The ordination of women

Should the ordained leadership include women? This is not the same as asking whether women can be included in the leadership team of a local church. On that there can be little room for debate in view of the good evidence which exists of women exercising a share in leadership in the early church before the development of a cultic priestly ministry.[14] If corporate leadership is a principle underlying the varying practice of the early church, then that principle can hardly be fully operative without the distinctive gifts which women have to contribute. But can women bear the representative authority which is given to the ordained ministry?

The question is customarily debated in terms of a cultic priesthood. For example, in an exchange of correspondence between Lambeth and the Vatican between December 1984 and June 1986 arguments were advanced on the one hand that the priesthood, in order to be fully representative of the humanity which was redeemed in Christ, must include both the male and the female; while on the other side it was asserted that Christ is male in order to be the Head, while the church is female in order to be the Bride in the economy of salvation:

The priest represents Christ in His saving relationship with His Body the Church. He does not primarily represent the priesthood of the whole people of God. However unworthy, the priest stands *in persona Christi*. Christ's saving sacrifice is made present in the world as a sacramental reality in and through the ministry of priests.'[15]

This extreme expression of a cultic view of Christianity essentially removes any proper priesthood from the laity. But the church's leadership is not meant to be a priesthood of that kind. Women already belong to the church's priesthood by virtue of their baptism.

The question of the ordination of women is to be determined, on the charismatic view of authority put forward in this chapter, not according to sex but according to gifts. It is the ascended Christ who gives gifts of leadership to the church. It is therefore highly relevant to note that there are increasing numbers of women who believe that they are called to serve the church in this way. The possibility that this belief stems from an arrogant spirit of self-advancement is intrinsically no more likely than in the case of men who also confess to a sense of vocation in this direction. Both alike must be subject to the church's testing and confirmation of their call. But the church has no warrant for saying that in the case of women such a vocation can never exist.[16]

The leadership of deacons

All ministry is service. Most of all, leadership in the gospel community is a ministry of humble service for the welfare of all, following the essential pattern provided for the church by Christ himself (Lk 22:27). Down the ages ordained ministry has gathered so much status that it is commonly seen on a higher plane altogether than lay ministry. The ministry of the laity as the true Christian priesthood is quite overshadowed by the small minority who compose the clergy, who have spent on them an overwhelming proportion of the funds raised to train and to maintain the church's ministry, and who are accorded priority in dignity in the church's ceremonies, and rights of veto in the church's government.

Amongst the clergy, from the earliest origins of ordained ministry, has existed an order of deacons. There is much confusion and uncertainty over how the basic word for ministry in the New Testament came to be applied to a particular order. In subsequent history deacons have become either trainee priests or else lay officers, since it was difficult to understand how anyone called to holy orders could find fulfilment in being a mere deacon. It will be suggested in a later chapter that leadership in the local church might be strengthened by having a team of deacons in addition to a team of elders. At this point the gospel paradox of having servants who are leaders will be used to make the comment that leadership in the church can never be an exclusive thing. The structures we create may make it appear so, but in the gospel community we are all called to be deacons, for, as Sir Thomas More once said, 'God hath given to every man cure and charge of his neighbour.'

Part three: Grounds for hope

7: The changing scene

Theory and practice since 1945

Over the last forty years there has been, firstly, a growing emphasis on ministry as the ministry of the whole church, and secondly, a realization that in the early church, and in most rapidly growing churches today, the local leadership is both corporate and indigenous.

Movement has been surprisingly slow, considering the weight of the arguments and the pressures from falling numbers in the full-time professional ministry being felt in many denominations. This slow progress has been partly due to the resistance to change natural in any long-established institution, and partly to the emphasis on the centrality of the building, the priest and the services, described in earlier chapters. These factors have perhaps particularly affected the Church of England and the Roman Catholic Church, where the professional minister was more thoroughly and totally separated from the people than in other denominations. More important, however, has been the sad fact that until recently almost all churches assumed that adult Christian education ended after confirmation and membership instruction, with the result that there have not been enough lay people available with the capacity and the confidence to play the more active role now being expected of them.

1.The ministry of the whole church

In the 1950's Yves Congar and other Roman Catholic theologians began to write about the laity as the whole people of God, and to challenge the traditional understanding of the priesthood. Congar noted, for example, the complete absence of the word 'priest' from both the New Testament and the Apostolic Fathers, as a description of the church's ministers. He noted the continuation of 'lay presbyters' in Africa up to at least the fourth century. He pointed out that alternative forms of church activity – cells, communities, conferences, clubs, camps and societies of all kinds – had throughout history usually emerged as a result of the inspiration and leadership of lay people, and often as part of a protest against the rigidity of the established and clerically dominated structures.

At the same time Hendrik Kraemer and others in European Protestant churches were beginning to say that the main part of the ministry of the clergy should be to enable the laity to fulfil their lay ministry. The laity were the front-line troops, but were almost totally untrained for the battle! A revolution in thinking was required. Kraemer wrote, 'When a church has for ages kept its members in a state of spiritual immaturity, they cannot suddenly be expected to function as spiritual adults'. He called for a 'fearless scrutiny and revision of structures, as one of the most urgent aspects of renewal in the church'[1].

This argument was given more detailed biblical backing by the publication in 1960 of Paul Minear's *Images of the Church in the New Testament*, based on work commissioned by the Faith and Order Department of the World Council of Churches. From his detailed analysis of every word or phrase used to describe the church (over 100 different items), Minear drew out four 'master-images': the people of God, the new creation, the fellowship of faith, and the body of Christ. He indicated the danger of selecting any one of these images on its own as a foundation for discussing the nature of the church, and he stressed that all four were pictures of the whole church, and not of any part of it. The church is a corporate body, whose corporate purpose is both priestly and ministerial. If status is ever mentioned, it is the status of the whole body, not of any part of it, and that status is always linked with a purpose or function. The church is chosen and redeemed in order to serve and witness. The 'whole church participates in the one ministry of Christ to the world', and none of the New Testament images provides any justification for clericalism.[2]

At a more popular level, discussion was opened up widely by the publication in 1964 of *God's Frozen People* by Mark Gibbs and T Ralph Morton. They stressed the absolute necessity for every-member ministry, and therefore the need for lay Christians to be better educated and trained for their great variety of ministry, both in church and world. They continued to challenge the almost universal assumption of clerical domination which underlay so much of the current practice of all the churches, and perhaps particularly of the Church of England.

2. *The growing call for corporate and indigenous local leadership*

The cry for more clergy has always gone up when numbers coming forward for ordination have been low, and early attempts to develop some form of auxiliary or supplementary ministry, particularly in the Church of England, sprang mainly from this concern. The very word 'auxiliary' demonstrates that they were seen primarily as assistants, or gap-fillers. But there was also a growing body of opinion calling for something very different. Both theological and practical arguments pointed to the need for the sort of indigenous ministry which Roland Allen had pressed for so strongly in the missionary provinces. His *Missionary Methods – St Paul's or Ours?* (1912) was reprinted seven times between 1953 and 1962, as people suddenly saw the relevance of what he had written forty to fifty years before. This had very wide influence, through the as yet unanswered case it made for the natural local leadership of the local church to be ordained.

The Southwark Ordination Course, seen by many at first as 'a piece of bold and dangerous pioneering', was set up in 1960 against this background, so that local men could be trained without having to leave their jobs to go to college. Much was made at first of the fact that a number of 'ordinary working men' were ordained as a result. But church authorities were anxious to avoid any possibility of allegations about 'second-class clergy' so they insisted that the quality of spare-time training should be comparable with that at the full-time training colleges. Unfortunately the only measure of quality available was the academic one. As a result, training on a spare-time basis proved in many respects to be even more demanding than residential training. The report, *Non-Stipendiary Ministry in the Church of England* shows that in fact the part-time training courses, now seventeen in number, have almost totally failed in their original purpose of opening up the ordained ministry to people from all walks of life. No less than thirty-eight per cent of the men ordained NSM between 1971 and 1981 had been teachers or lecturers when they started training for ordination, and the overwhelming majority of the others had been in professional, managerial or administrative posts.[3]

Neither Roland Allen nor the later supporters of indigenous leadership seem to have caught hold of the fact that indigenous leadership also has to be corporate. This principle of corporate leadership was underlined by AT Hanson in his book, *Pioneer Ministry* (1961). He demonstrated that even the apostle Paul, the epitome of a dynamic leader and pioneer, always operated with a team, rather than on his own; that the local leadership of the early church was always a team of presbyters or overseers, rather than one presbyter on his own; and that this local leadership is properly defined by its function, in relation to the church and the gospel, rather than by its validity, authority or status. Indeed, its only status must be that of *diakonos* or servant, the word being applied equally to Christ, to the apostles, to local church leaders, and to every member. All are called to serve, none are to 'lord it over others'; but within each local church, some of its members are given the particular role of pastors and teachers, to enable and equip the whole local church for the work of ministry.[4] At a more popular level, this was also the theme of *Called to Serve* by Michael Green (1964). Theologian Jim Packer, addressing a conference on Ministry in the church in 1965, called for the 'sweeping away of current misconceptions of the ministry (the focus on one man working on his own) . . . and the recognition of lay eldership'. Before long some of the seeds being sown in this way began to germinate.

3. Early experiments in the Church of England

The first pioneers of local eldership emerged in the late sixties. After a period of consultation, study and preparation initiated by Roy Henderson, Vicar of St Luke's, Barton Hill, Bristol, the Bishop of Bristol laid a hand on six laymen 'to carry out the office of Elder in this congregation'. These men were described in *Ministry in the Seventies* as 'the natural leaders of the local church, whose moral and spiritual qualifications fitted those required by the Pastoral Epistles'. They had a 'sufficient knowledge of the Bible, a love for the Lord, and Christian characters that had stood the test of time' but lacked the academic capacity to participate in training for what was then called Auxiliary Pastoral Ministry, even if a local course had been available. There was no question of ordination, at least in the terms in which ordination was then understood.[5]

Other essays in *Ministry in the Seventies* took up this theme. Bill Persson, later Bishop of Doncaster, called for real participation by lay leaders in the spiritual responsibility and decision-making of the parish. Colin Brown underlined the New Testament pattern of 'several bishops in every local church', and stressed the evidence that the only form of local leadership known to the New Testament writers was corporate. Tim Dudley-Smith, later Bishop of Thetford, called for lay elders or lay pastors to be ordained as a recognized supplementary ministry, corporate, local, and not necessarily lifelong, selected for their character and spirituality, not their academic ability. David Sheppard, later Bishop of Liverpool, argued that if the leadership structures were to 'revert from our one presbyter to the New Testament pattern of presbyters (plural) in a shared ministry, this would make it possible to develop the local working-class clergy so badly needed in industrial areas'. This last idea was already becoming a reality in Bethnal Green in London's East End. In *Partners and Ministers* (1972), Ted Roberts described the background of thinking and discussion and the wholly local training programme, lasting five years, which led to four local men from two parishes being ordained to the Auxiliary Pastoral Ministry by Trevor Huddleston, Bishop of Stepney in 1974. This was seen as a deliberate attempt to create a local team of ordained elders on New Testament lines, as opposed to the much more individual basis which was normal in APM at the time. The aim was to create a local team, called by the local church, trained locally, settled rather than itinerant, voluntary not paid, and not necessarily lifelong.[6]

The lay eldership experiment at Bristol was at first successful, but two of the key members quite soon moved away and three others died within a short period. Although one or two were added to the team later, the experiment gradually lost momentum and petered out, as it was not always possible to replace the losses. The more ambitious Bethnal Green experiment also suffered from being a pioneer – far ahead of the general thinking of the church, and trying to squeeze into a five-year period a whole range of changed expectations.

Both Barton Hill and Bethnal Green were working-class

areas. One lesson learned in both places and confirmed elsewhere is the vital need in such places for a really long-term commitment by the professional minister if a local team is to be securely established. The whole process of being selected and trained inevitably 'distances' local team members somewhat from their fellow church members, and also from their local culture. They have to read more, they work with a diary, they begin to take on extra responsibilities. Ordination gives them a new status in the eyes of the local church and neighbourhood, and places on them extra expectations of authority and extra demands on their time. To cope with this they need the continuing pastoral and administrative support upon which they have come to depend during their training. The departure of the minister who built up the team seems to be more disruptive here than it would be in other cultural contexts.

An experiment somewhat similar to Bethnal Green emerged in Southwark Diocese in 1980. In the Brandon scheme four local men from four adjacent parishes which were beginning to work together were trained locally, with their clergy participating in most of their training. But although they trained as a team, their subsequent work has been very much as individuals, assisting their vicars in much the same way as would an ordinary NSM trained in the normal way. Both these experiments demonstrated the feasibility of local training and ordination for those without normal academic qualifications, but neither experiment created a team of presbyters within a single parish.

Local ordained ministry has been slow to get off the ground. But the pioneers have helped pave the way for its official development in a number of dioceses under guidelines approved by the Bishops. This looks as if it may lead at last to the sort of local clergy in local teams for which so many have been calling, and further impetus has been given by the report on urban priority areas, *Faith in the City* (1985)[7]. The Barton Hill experiment of lay elders, however, has an increasing number of imitations, of great variety, some of which are included in the survey described in the next chapter.

An experiment on rather different lines also began in the late sixties in the largely rural diocese of St Edmundsbury and Ipswich. The sharp fall in clergy numbers meant that three or four parishes, and sometimes more, were having to share a vicar. Lay elders were therefore set up as a focus of pastoral care in each village, and as a pastoral link between the parish and the vicar. Over the years the number involved has grown steadily and instead of one lay elder in each place, the emphasis is now increasingly on developing a local team.

4. Baptist, House Church and URC elders

The same movement away from the traditional one-man ministry has been a steadily increasing feature in most other denominations. In many Baptist and other independent evangelical churches – where the pastor or Minister was often as much on his own and as dominant as any vicar – elders have recently been appointed. Usually they are chosen from within the existing team of deacons. In a few cases the diaconate as such has ceased to exist, following the appointment of elders. Its administrative and financial functions are then exercised by two or three individuals. In others, the diaconate as a whole has taken on the eldership role of sharing in the pastoral and spiritual oversight and leadership, retaining its traditional title but handing on its traditional functions to a new committee.

More often the result has been that a sort of 'three-fold ministry' has developed within a single local church, very much as seems to have been the pattern in the second century in the early days of episcopacy. In one large Baptist church this whole three-fold structure is called the Diaconate. It consists of the Pastor – full time, professional and clearly recognized as the presiding elder; the lay elders whose role is to share in the pastoral oversight and leadership; and the deacons, who continue to be responsible for finance, administration and buildings.

Elders were originally a common feature of Baptist constitutions in the seventeenth century. More recently, 'elder' had become a merely honorary title, often used as a synonym for 'life-deacon' when the time came for an elderly deacon to be 'put out to grass'.

Fresh thinking among Baptists was on very similar lines to that of Anglicans. In *The Pattern of the Church* (1963) for example, one of the main requirements of local church leadership, that is, pastoral care, was seen as being beyond the capacity of one man: 'those with special responsibility for administration will be called deacons; those with special responsibility in pastoral care will be called elders'.[8] Not long afterwards, the Baptist report, *Ministry Tomorrow* called for supplementary Ministers to be trained and recognized, particularly for the pastoral charge of smaller churches which could not afford a paid minister. It was emphasized that this would only work properly if the part-time Minister were part of a team of local church elders. Both documents emphasized the importance of local calling and recognition of those with the appropriate pastoral gifts to be elders, and also of appropriate training to be available, without which it would be more difficult to overcome the reluctance of congregations to accept pastoral ministry from an amateur.

This pattern is also very much part of the still-developing House Church or Community Church movement. Within the variety of leadership styles of the different networks, and the varying degree of authority exercised from outside by those whom they recognize as 'apostles' or by the first generation leaders, the normal pattern is to have a team of elders in each local congregation. Often the local elders are at first unpaid, and do the work in their spare time; as numbers grow, they then call one or more of their elders into part-time or full-time employment.

In some house-church networks training is available. Often the men involved have had some bible-college training previously, some have been trained for the pastorate, and some have been pastors already. But many house-church elders, like those in Baptist congregations, are simply men with the appropriate gifts whose abilities have emerged through sharing in leadership of house-groups or other kinds of pastoral responsibility. They are then recognized publicly by their congregations, normally with the involvement of some kind of external representative. This approach is in line with that of many of the rapidly growing independent churches overseas, whose normal practice is 'to ordain only middle-aged men, of proven integrity, experience and ability', to work together as a team of local elders.[9] This is seen as appropriate to churches of all sizes.

A later report from the Baptist Union entitled *Half the Denomination* argues the need for shared leadership even in the churches of less than fifty members (which represent forty-eight per cent of Baptist congregations) on the basis that an effective ministry is most likely to be built up when the need for several part-time participants is fully accepted, each contributing on a limited basis, but all working together in a consciously planned partnership.

In the United Reformed Church, as in the Church of Scotland, elders are part of the system. Here too, however, there has been a growing concern in recent years to draw the elders, or at least some of them, into a deeper sharing with the Minister in the overall responsibility for the whole life of the church and to question the adequacy of the tradition of giving each elder a 'district' or list of up to a dozen families to be visited two or three times each year.

Life and Work, the monthly journal of the Church of Scotland, carried a series of articles on eldership in 1984/85. 'We need to review, if not reconstruct, our ideas of eldership; the elders should be seen as sharing with the Minister in leadership and in other responsibilities; they should be a spiritual 'management team', assessing priorities, making policy decisions, initiating action, monitoring results, but above all visionary, seeking to discern God's purposes for his church here today'. There was a repeated emphasis on the two-fold task of the elders: serving needs within the congregation and enabling the congregation to serve the world. Many wanted to see much deeper participation by the elders in leading worship, in the spiritual nurture of the congregation, and in the overall pastoral oversight. Several contributors saw that this would require much more training for effective eldership. Some also saw a renewed eldership as the main recruiting ground for the full-time ministry. Why should not candidates be selected and sponsored by the congregation among whom they have already worked and served for a number of years? In this way their witness to their faith and their fitness to minister would have been tried and tested among a real fellowship through real situations over a period of time.

5. *Roman Catholic thinking*

In a very remarkable way this line of thought is precisely mirrored in much unofficial Roman Catholic thinking and writing, from almost every continent. From the totally different setting of Tanzania, American Roman Catholic missionary Vincent Donovan describes in *Christianity Rediscovered* (1982) the conversion to Christ of several Masai villages which he had been visiting for a year. By the time they were ready for baptism, he could already see those who were the 'natural priests and spiritual leaders in their community', those who had the gift of leading worship, for explaining the gospel, for enabling the young Christian community to live and grow. But these local men and women – married, often illiterate, gifted by the Holy Spirit, and already functioning in the New Testament sense as leaders, elders and teachers in the church – could not be ordained. Donovan points to the utter inappropriateness of expecting an urbanized, educated seminary-trained Masai priest to become what their own natural and spiritual leaders already were.[10]

This point was also made by another American Roman Catholic, Stephen Clark, co-ordinator of the Word of God Christian Community in Ann Arbor, Michigan. He says ordination will be most effective when those ordained are the natural leaders of the Christian people. He argues the case for a completely new approach to leadership in the church: a team, rather than a single priest, mainly composed of those already demonstrating their capacity to help create the sort of community which will enable all its members to live a vital Christian life in the world. 'The church needs men who are committed to Christ above all, and who are willing to work to bring others to a committment to Him' – and then to build them up into maturity. No one man can be expected to cope on his own with the great variety of problems and to create the supportive atmosphere within which people's gifts can develop. The process of real growth cannot get off the ground without a team.[11]

These examples reflect the wave of new thinking in the Roman Catholic church, particularly since Vatican II. In many countries they have seen an even sharper decline in vocations to the priesthood than other denominations, and in many developing countries where marriage is part of the cultural norm the requirement of celibacy means that vocations hardly exist. A married diaconate is now increasingly common, and many places now have considerable experience of regular worship led by deacons, nuns, and lay people. But there are deeper reasons for change than decline in numbers. Only in the last forty years have ordinary Catholics been positively encouraged to read the Bible. This has led many to begin to question tradition. In the last twenty years the charismatic renewal movement has transformed the way many churches live and work at the grass roots. The rigid official position of the church on ordination to the priesthood has not yet changed; but it surely cannot resist much longer the combination of grass roots pressure, practical needs, and the theological arguments put forward by Kung, Rahner, Schillebeeckx and others.

Kung, for example, argues that leadership in the church is not necessarily full-time, professional, or lifelong, does not require celibacy, nor is it essentially wholly masculine, but it does require the gifts of enabling and co-ordinating the gifts of others. Ordination should be seen as the church calling publicly those it believes God has already called and gifted, legitimating both to them and to their community their calling to leadership.[12] Schillebeeckx and others have argued that leadership in the local Christian community was for the first thousand years the normal foundation for ordination, and that this is still appropriate today. They see the primary function of the ordained ministry as preaching, teaching, and leading the community. The presidency at the eucharist is the natural consequence of those primary tasks. Schillebeeckx describes the current official understanding of priesthood as 'the ossification of a church order of past centuries which is now an obstacle to what it was originally designed to achieve'.[13] This ossification is at the heart of the church's current problems: 'a passive laity, omnicompetent clergy, a regression to Old Testament models of priesthood, irrelevant priorities at high level'[14]. The cry in many places is for the ordination to a local ministry of the recognized spiritual leaders of the local community. The wider church 'has to test such leaders in regard to their suitability; it may or even must train them . . . but the qualities required for such a local leader . . . must be related to *this* basic community and its current situation'.[15]

6. The ministry of deacons
In addition to this clearly identified movement in almost all denominations towards some form of corporate local eldership, there has also been a widespread but much less clearly focused desire, particularly in the older denominations, for a revived diaconate.

Recent tradition
In most episcopal churches, until very recently, the diaconate had become simply a probationary year before virtually automatic ordination to the presbyterate, but in the last thirty years this has increasingly come under attack. Some have argued from the practical standpoint that there was 'diaconal' work to be done for which people needed official recognition. This included those who stressed the pastoral/parish worker ministry of deaconesses and others who wished to sweep into a single

group all the full-time lay employees of the church, from diocesan administrators to youth, social and community workers. Others have seen the need for a diaconate which could in principle at least be lifelong, if the three-fold ministry of bishop, presbyter and deacon was to be commended seriously to other churches as a basis for unity. Others, observing that present Anglican practice bears no relation either to biblical or to early church precedent, have suggested that the diaconate be abolished.

In many of the Reformation churches the liturgical element of the deacons' original role disappeared, while their pastoral and administrative functions developed in a number of different ways. Some churches have given them a major role in decision-making; in others, their main task is financial; in some European churches deacons and deaconesses are in full-time Christian social work, as individuals or as part of a community. Some churches have no deacons at all.

There is little guidance on a renewed diaconate in either the World Council of Churches Report, *Baptism Eucharist & Ministry* (BEM) or indeed in the ARCIC *Statement on Ministry*. The BEM commentary notes the 'widespread uncertainty on the status and function of the diaconate' and asks in what sense are deacons part of the ordained ministry? The text then describes deacons as 'exemplifying the interdependence of worship and service in the church's life . . . in reading the scriptures . . . preaching . . . teaching . . . exercising a ministry of love within the community; . . . fulfilling certain administrative tasks . . . and may be elected to responsibilities for governance'!

The ARCIC report sets the scene very fairly: 'Within the New Testament, ministerial actions are varied and functions not precisely defined . . . but with the growth of the church the importance of certain functions led to their being located in specific officers of the community'. But the reference to deacons is remarkably unhelpful: ' . . . they are associated with bishops and presbyters in the ministry of the word and sacrament, and assist in oversight'. Any churchwarden who is also a Reader could be described in that way![16]

BEM and ARCIC could be summed up as saying, 'deacons can assist bishops and presbyters in any way that is agreed to be appropriate, including sharing in responsibility, but they cannot absolve, celebrate or ordain'.

Roman Catholic developments

The permanent diaconate was restored by Pope Paul in 1967, and in many countries there was a ready response, in marked contrast to the almost universal decline in vocations to the priesthood. By 1975 in the USA there were 800 permanent deacons; by 1980, 4,656 had been ordained and 2,514 were in training.[17]

Their work is very varied. Some work mainly within the congregations (pastoral), some mainly in the outside world (charitable) with the young, the old, the sick, the disabled, the handicapped and the poor, with action and community groups, orphanages, hospices and so on. Some are full-time and paid, but not all. There is a measure of ambivalence in their status, with official insistence on the diaconate as a lower-grade 'sacred order' alongside a desire that they should have no special dress and should not use the title 'Reverend'. There is a positive emphasis on working as a team, rather than as individuals: 'a body of deacons in a parish could not only relieve the overwhelming burden borne by the clergy but would multiply the effective ministry of the church both among its own people and in the community'.[18]

In much of the third world, where vocations to the priesthood have been even scarcer, Roman Catholic deacons are now doing virtually everything that a priest would be expected to do, in running parishes and giving teaching and pastoral care to the congregations.

Anglican confusion

In the Anglican Communion progress has been very much slower, partly due to divided views on whether a revived diaconate should be a 'lay' or a 'holy order', and to strong clerical opposition to allowing women into a holy order at all. It is sad that status should be so crucial an issue when the whole emphasis of diaconal ministry is to have no status at all other than that of servant. Deaconesses themselves have been graciously willing to submit to whatever procedures for 'ordination' the church sees fit to impose upon them. The Anglican Consultative Council in 1976, while agreeing that the diaconate should continue to be seen as a period of probation for the priesthood, went on to ask member churches 'to examine the concept of the diaconate as an order to which lay people serving the church, or serving in the name of the church, could also be admitted, to express and convey the authority of the church in their service'. This has not wholly clarified the problem. Many people do not want a clericalized diaconate, but others insist that the diaconate is a holy order; others still are confused about where to draw the line between those who serve church or world within the diaconate, and those who do identical work without any such official recognition. The ACC in 1984 encouraged the process of discussion to continue, but unfortunately seems to have abandoned the parochial emphasis which is so strong in Roman Catholic thinking. 'We see the diaconate as a ministry to the poor . . . to be exercised directly under the bishop [and presumably therefore on the central diocesan payroll?], seeking with him to interpret to the church the needs, concerns and hopes of those the deacon is called to serve'. They noted that 'in dioceses where the diaconate is being reviewed the deacon is found in some cases in the lay order and in others within the clergy order,' and call for further study to be done in this area.

The way forward

The one thing clear from this brief summary is that there is a general desire for a real diaconate in all the churches, but no common mind as to the form or forms it should take. This confusion may be due to a failure to identify properly a key biblical principle. In Acts chapter 6, and generally throughout the New Testament, the emphasis is on differentiation of functions within the recognized local ministry of the church. For example, the Seven were very definitely *not* appointed to help the apostles with their work, but rather themselves to take on certain necessary work which the apostles should not have been expected to do, and which was in practice preventing them doing the work they had been called to do. [19] In the epistles, whether we look at lists of gifts or at references to different types of work, the emphasis is very much on each person doing that which he or she is equipped by God to do, in order that the church may grow and the needs of all may be met. It has been well said that 'the needs of the church [and its work] should dictate the shape of its ministry'. In the Jerusalem church there was clearly a need to take certain specific burdens off the shoulders of the church leaders, and it is not surprising that a similar pattern developed elsewhere, and included the appointment of female deacons. [20] In any contemporary culture, it would have been quite inappropriate for men to be involved in the pastoral visiting of women, and in preparing them for baptism. By the early second century, it seems that deacons and elders (both plural) were a normal feature of every local church. The deacons received offerings of cash or in kind at the eucharist, and distributed them to the poor, as indeed they distributed the bread at the eucharist itself. There was therefore a strong link in those early days between their roles in worship, in finance, and in pastoral care. Professor Lampe has suggested that the effectiveness of the early diaconate contributed greatly to the growth of Christianity, as 'paganism could not match its concern for the relief of the poor and needy'.[21] Many believe that the same could be true today.

8: How some churches have established corporate leadership

During the last ten years a steadily increasing number of churches of all denominations have begun to move towards some form of shared, corporate, local pastoral leadership. Although some have run into painful problems on the way, which will be looked at in the next chapter, virtually everyone is convinced that this is the right way to go, in spite of the many difficulties and pressures that may be encountered; this includes those whose experiments have failed.

Widespread evidence

The evidence which follows is based upon personal visits in 1983 to 155 different churches. In most cases these entailed an hour and a half with the Vicar, Minister or Pastor; in about thirty cases some or all of the local team were involved, sometimes without their Minister. These visits were followed up two years later by letter and telephone, to discover how each local situation had developed.

The sample was collected initially by writing to church newspapers and by contacting home missionary society secretaries and diocesan officials, and this produced a preliminary list of places to be visited. But almost every visit led to further suggestions, and the number grew so fast that it proved impossible to investigate all of them in the time available.

The churches visited were well spread both by denomination and geographically, and included 110 Anglican, eighteen Baptist, ten Brethren and Independent, six Methodist, five House Church, four Roman Catholic and two URC. Of these, sixty-five were in southern England, forty-two north of a line between the Wash and the Dee and forty-five in between. They were of all sizes: sixty claimed a main service attendance of between 100 and 250 adults, fifty less than 100 and forty-five more than 250. They were well mixed in type of area, including affluent middle-class suburban, working class/ owner-occupied, council estates, inner-city, city centre, small town and rural parishes. But the largest group was that which described its neighbourhood as socially mixed. Their churchmanship varied considerably, although more than half were evangelical; of the others, many would reckon that contact with the charismatic renewal movement had played a part in the process of leading them towards change. Most of them had only been involved in 'shared leadership' for a relatively short time. In sixty churches the team had only started within the previous five years; in another twenty-five the beginning was between 1974 and 1978; only five had had any sort of team before then. The other sixty-five could not give a precise date for when the team had begun. It had emerged so gradually over a period of years that it was difficult to give a date. Out of the eight earliest teams only two were still in operation.

The variety in their approach

These 155 very different churches had approached the idea of corporate leadership for various reasons and in several different ways. Their emerging teams have developed in different ways as well. A number of critical factors appear to lie behind this variety:

• The gifts and personality of the Minister; his vision for the church, his own ability to develop and to lead a team; in particular, his willingness to share and to delegate.

• The gifts of those with formally recognized positions in the church – churchwardens, deacons and readers.

• The availability of gifts lying dormant within the congregation, often unused because unrecognized.

• The character of the congregation itself and the extent to which it is tied and bound by traditional expectations or open to the implications of new thinking; and whether its members already have a sense of belonging together and of being the church.

• The numerical size of the congregation, and the

geographical compactness and cohesion (or otherwise) of its catchment area.

It is possible to identify four main ways in which churches move towards corporate leadership. The starting point can be: (i) a pastoral team; (ii) a consultative group; (iii) a management team or (iv) a pastoral leadership team, sometimes called an eldership. Although these approaches sometimes overlap and the situation is often further complicated because teams can move from one approach to another in a short space of time, it is worth attempting to analyse the four approaches separately, not least because problems frequently occur when the team is in the process of moving from one approach to another without realizing what is happening or understanding the consequences which can arise from such a process, both for themselves and for the rest of the church.

1.The pastoral team
Purpose and variety
In places where there is no tradition or experience of shared ministry, the pastoral team seems to be the simplest and most common starting-point. A few examples will illustrate the variety of ways in which such a team can come into being.

Where it is a case of starting completely from scratch, the Minister can simply gather together a small team to help him with visiting. He spends time with them, more or less regularly, allocating visits and advising on problems encountered. They pray together. Some start simply by delivering an invitation to a special service or the regular church newsletter. In some places door-to-door visiting for a whole area of the parish is still possible and useful. Other teams visit the sick and those in need – both those who belong to the church and those who turn to the church in times of crisis. Some teams visit newcomers, or a newly-developed housing estate. The aim may be just to make friendly contact, or to respond to known needs. Or it may be the case that there is no known need, but the team visits to build up the strength of the fellowship, and discover and develop the gifts members possess.

Pastoral teams have been set up in places where it had been previously assumed that the Vicar did everything, in situations as diverse as rural Dorset and East Anglia, a Yorkshire housing estate, and a parish of 50,000 on the outskirts of Birmingham with only one full-time clergyman. In this last case, the Vicar began by recruiting five women with school-age children and with the right sort of personality, each of whom was willing to undertake two or three visits a week. Additions to the team have only just kept pace with departures: three left simply because they found they hadn't time to do it properly, one went into full-time work, and two others have taken on part-time social work. Overall, even on this small scale, the result has been more visiting, more pastoral care in the name of the church; and this vast parish is slowly getting used to the idea that the church is very much more than the Vicar.

A team like this can develop into something not unlike the eldership in a United Reformed Church. Each member can be given responsibility for anything from six to twenty homes, which they then visit and make contact with in other ways on a regular basis.

One large church in South London has a team of sixty men and women called 'Pastors', each with a responsibility for visiting eight or ten individuals (which usually includes one other member of the visiting team). They aim to visit and pray with those on their list three times a year, and to know them well enough to be aware of any special need. They were orig-inally selected by the Vicar with his five Readers, invited by letter to serve, and given an initial briefing. This is supplemented by an occasional training evening and an annual personal interview, and the whole operation is now co-ordi-nated by a lay volunteer.

In one large and mixed Midland parish the entire electoral roll of about 200 was divided among a team of five on an alphabetical basis which, they said, was the easiest way to save argument! The team committed themselves to a home visit once a year, and to maintaining personal contact as necessary at other times.

In a number of Anglican churches which are part of official Team Ministries, the whole District Church Council shares the pastoral care of the whole congregational list.[1] One Team Vicar claimed that this would not work with a PCC because of its formal responsibilities, but that it was ideal for the fifteen members of his DCC, with 150 in the congregation. Each member of the Council, with ten adults to contact, was able to visit four times a year to deliver the newsletter, and was committed to pray for those on their list.

Training and team support

In many cases, training for these teams depends at least initially upon the Minister. It is vital for him to make time available on a continuing basis for the members of the team as a group and also as individuals, both to make best use of their potential and to detect and deal with any emerging problems. When people are given responsibility, they often grow in Christian maturity and begin to feel a deeper concern for the people they are visiting and for the life of the local church. They discover the real needs of church members and the community. Some may want to get more involved, and in their regular meeting with the Minister they find themselves making plans and taking decisions in areas which in fact lie outside their initial brief. This growth in responsibility and concern can easily become a problem if it leads to crossed wires with the normal decision-making bodies in the church. The pastoral team finds itself not only acting like a pastoral committee of the Church Council, but actually usurping some of its tasks.

Equally serious problems occur when team members find they cannot cope with the responsibility thrust upon them. As people discover their willingness to help, their telephones and doorbells ring more frequently and pressure on their home and family life increases. This often happens before they have developed the internal resources necessary to cope – the pastoral experience, the spiritual maturity, and the ability to sometimes say 'No'! If at the same time they are not getting sufficient external support, they may even break down and give up – and the consequences of this can be a serious sense of guilt and failure. The Minister has to find time for the personal support of his pastoral team. At the same time the congregation has to learn how much it can reasonably expect from them!

The Diocese of Ely, which specifically promotes the development of these pastoral teams, sees team support as essential. In some Ely parishes the fact that team members are known as elders has caused confusion, and many would prefer the title of Lay Pastoral Assistants, which is certainly a more accurate description and is also widely used elsewhere. But whatever the title, these teams have made possible a real increase in the volume of pastoral visiting, and many congregations are slowly getting used to the idea. People are becoming more willing to talk seriously with someone other than the full-time ordained

Minister, and in the words of one Ely Vicar, 'many team members are discovering gifts they never dreamed they had'.

Jimmy Hamilton-Brown, one of the early promotors of lay eldership, moved to Dorchester in 1982. He at once began the process of recruiting a pastoral team of ten couples in the parish church, training them himself. Two years later the other two churches in his Dorchester Team Ministry sent members on to the new twelve-week course for Lay Pastoral Assistants, run locally by the Diocese, which offers a basic introduction to pastoral work.

Training schemes like this are becoming more widely available across the country, and although they are all very new, three clear conclusions are already emerging. First, the fact that 'ordinary people like us' can go on a course and be used in the work of the church in various ways often makes it easier to encourage others in the congregation to become involved. Secondly, many of those who complete the initial basic course want to go back before long for something more demanding and probably more specialized. Thirdly, many people discover that the fact that they have had some form of training, however limited in depth, and have been authorized or commissioned in some way, enables them to go visiting with greater confidence and also means that they are received more readily. In this last area, however, there must be great sensitivity in not down-grading the visiting and other caring work often being done by other members of the congregation, who for whatever reason may not be able to attend a training course. Any sense of élitism must be avoided. Every member of the church is called and authorized to 'minister', in the sense of caring for and loving each other and their neighbours, simply on the basis of baptism – 'soldiers and servants of Christ' to the end of their lives. Those who go on a course are trying to equip themselves to do this more effectively, and perhaps also to do it officially in the name of the church.

In many cases people find that even after a very general and basic training course, either their gifts or the local needs lead them into particular areas of work, and away from general pastoral visiting. In one council housing estate parish, for example, the first four who trained on the Wakefield Shared Ministry Project each discovered different priorities. One visited regularly with the parish magazine, one helped to follow up all baptism contacts, one concentrated on visiting newcomers and another shared in visiting the sick and elderly. Often these people find themselves being drawn into traditional church jobs – helping with Sunday School or youth work, becoming a churchwarden, or helping to start a housegroup. As they become more aware of the needs of the church and the local community they see the need for new activities, or for more help with existing church activities. This means that there is a continuing need to recruit new members for the Pastoral Visiting Team, and to promote this as an effective way of developing shared ministry in the widest possible sense.

In larger churches it may be possible to develop several different specialized pastoral teams. One church in Leeds, for example, has a team of about fifteen people visiting the sick, elderly, housebound and those in hospital, and a smaller team visiting new-comers to the parish and new contacts in the church. A church in Derby has a very large team of 'pastoral visitors' each of whom takes on responsibilities for one elderly person at a time. In addition it has a small team dealing with infant baptism follow-up (a three-year commitment) and is starting a team for bereavement visiting and another group to help with marriage preparation.

House group leaders as a pastoral team

With house groups now an increasingly frequent feature of church life, their leaders (and sometimes their members as well) are often a key element in local pastoral care. Many people believe they are also a vital factor in church growth, because the small group or cell is the level at which people can relate closely and personally to one another, to give and receive support, encouragement and the incentive to grow. Both learning and caring are easier in small groups.

House groups are of great variety – the emphasis may be on prayer, Bible study, discussion, or a specific area of concern and action, or they may be the sort of multi-purpose group which can almost be seen as a mini-church. If they are to grow healthily and avoid degenerating into cosy cliques, they need organized oversight. Their leaders need to meet regularly for training, preparation, and forward planning, as well as for mutual support and prayer. All too often this is given a low priority, with the result that many house groups are less effective than they could be.

In many churches the reason may well be that the house group leaders have other responsibilities as churchwardens, deacons or Readers. The Minister or his wife may also be leading a group. In small and medium-sized churches it is perfectly possible for the 'one-man ministry' to be replaced by the 'small group ministry', where an inner circle of keen and able people find themselves doing everything. They are the willing work horses who cheerfully shoulder every extra task, or more likely find themselves being pushed into it because no-one else is available. This can be thoroughly unsatisfactory, and it is important to diagnose the problem before everyone becomes too frustrated and before the groups start dying back from lack of care.

There are several ways of tackling this positively. The first essential is that planning should be in the context of the expectation of numerical growth. A static, maintenance only, 'at least we're keeping going' approach is not only stultifying, but also often prevents dormant gifts from emerging. Many churches have found the answer in sharing responsibilities for leadership of house groups. In addition, someone else may be the host, and someone else may act as the 'pastoral link' – a channel of communication with the Minister and between members of the group, which becomes almost essential if the group has been given a measure of pastoral responsibility for an area of the parish or a section of the congregational list. Finally, the leading of the Bible study/discussion/worship can be shared with others too, according to the gifts available, and if there seems to be no-one else able to undertake this, perhaps a thorough review of the way the groups are developing and how far they are meeting the needs of members is necessary.

Training leaders and planning for growth is costly in time required, and needs to be built into the programme from the beginning. In one church the Minister has for some years been meeting on a monthly basis with his ten house-group leaders to plan and pray for the life and growth of their groups. The Bible study in the other three weeks of the month is led in turn by three members of each group. Each of them attends a preparation evening during the week before it is his or her turn to lead. As a result no less than forty people out of a congregation of 200 are actually receiving regular once-a-month training in leading a group. Because the work is shared the risk of overloading is reduced to a minimum and the potential emergence of future group leaders (necessary in a highly mobile area) is maximized. The cost of this is one evening of the

Minister's time every week, on top of the time required for preparation of material, and for 'matters arising' from the weekly meetings.

This points to one key factor in promoting growth through groups. Many churches have discovered simply through experience that it is essential to appoint a specific person to oversee their growth and development, to minister to the group leaders, to help them evaluate progress and to help train assistant leaders. Without such oversight, it can be very difficult to move forward. With it, there is a greater chance that growth can be initiated and then sustained without anyone coming under excessive pressure.

Where there are only about half a dozen groups, one of the group leaders, or a deacon or Reader, or the Minister himself, may have the time and skill to do this job. But more often, and especially where the number of groups is greater, someone needs to be set free from other responsibilities in order to concentrate on this. Indeed, large churches with perhaps twenty or more house groups often have a team of house group co-ordinators or pastoral leaders under various titles, each of whom has the oversight of between three and six groups, with one of them co-ordinating the whole work.

Whatever the scale of the house group operation, the more alive the groups are, and the more positively they share in the pastoral life and work of the congregation, the greater becomes the need for close liaison between the clergy and the group leaders. They are beginning to share in the 'cure of souls' which every Vicar is given; they are acting as pastors and teachers of a small part of the congregation; they may be also becoming organizers of pastoral care on a wider basis. As their sense of responsibility deepens, people often find that their concern is spreading beyond the actual operation of their groups. 'How can our pattern of worship be improved? How can this person's gifts be trained and used? Who could take on that vital job? Why do so few of the congregation come from the housing estate which forms over half our population? What can we do to follow up newcomers?' Such widening concern can easily put too much pressure on the group leaders. It can also lead to their trespassing into the territory of the Church Council, in just the same way as a team of pastoral visitors in a small church which has begun to feel responsibility for the life and work of the church on a wider basis.

In both cases, what is happening is that the pastoral team, or some of its members, is beginning to move towards pastoral leadership. There is an emerging potential for developing some kind of corporate pastoral leadership or eldership (see p 97ff).

2. *The consultative group*

Some churches – mostly those with large and active congregations and many people already sharing in leadership of groups and organizations – have deliberately set up a small group for regular but informal consultation with the Minister. For example, one church with three worship centres, sixteen house groups and a host of other activities, where a previous pastoral leadership team had broken down, decided their next step must be to set up a temporary group to plan the way forward. It consisted of one (of four) churchwardens, two (of four) Readers, and the two clergy. The PCC confirmed its task and membership. In another church, following a twenty-five-year incumbency, the new Vicar set up a 'Vicar's advisory group' to share with him in forward planning, to discuss how to develop and use the considerable untapped resources of lay leadership, and to bring all its ideas and proposals regularly to the Church Council. In another church in a university city the churchwardens, two part-time clergy and the Vicar meet regularly as a co-ordinating group, sharing in forward thinking and consulting together on the best way of training and using their plentiful supply of lay leaders. In almost every case at least the majority of the team, if not all of it, are chosen from members of the Church Council, but in one unusual situation, where the parish had several separate congregations, the five members of the 'think-tank' group were specifically required *not* to be on the Church Council, and this seemed to be working well.

Some churches have deliberately kept this sort of group absolutely informal. Others have found it helpful to record its brief in a more formal way, however informally it is to function. One team was charged '(i) to act as support and stimulus to the Vicar in discerning what God is saying; (ii) to keep under review all proposals relating to mission and to suggest methods of implementing decisions.'

By far the commonest 'consultative group' however, might not even recognize itself as such. In a great number of churches the Minister takes counsel informally with a small group of those who already hold office in the church – such as church secretary, deacon, Reader or churchwarden. One Roman Catholic priest, with a recently established Church Council, reported that he 'never took any major decisions without consulting his elders', by which he meant four men each of whom already had an area of recognized responsibility in the life of the parish.

In all these situations the emphasis is on consultation, sharing the vision and forward thinking. This leads almost inevitably to sharing ideas about people, particularly those who might be asked to take on specific jobs in the church.

It can often be very simple and natural to set up a consultative group or think-tank, particularly when a new Minister comes to a church. Provided the church officers accept the idea, and if possible are involved themselves, no one is threatened. Such consultative groups seem sometimes to continue happily for years, as a useful soundingboard and support group for the Minister. But in many cases they seem to develop very naturally into something like the pastoral equivalent of the standing committee, or into being a pastoral leadership team or eldership. This can create problems in two ways. First, those involved may be excellent as a consultative group and may help clarify the vision of where the church should be going, but they may not have the skills or the time necessary for sharing effectively as a team in implementing the vision. Secondly, the borderline between taking counsel together and making decisions together is very easy to cross almost without noticing it. If this happens, there is at once a potential minefield of misunderstanding, with the Minister, the church officers and the team itself having differing expectations of their work together.

There is always the risk that a successful group of this kind will take on too much. This happened in a prosperous 300-strong Midlands church. There the group found it was reviewing past events and planning future events in some detail; discussing appointments of youth work helpers and house group leaders; sharing in planning the teaching programme; and reviewing church finances and missionary support. This overload had three consequences: they all knew they were not covering anything thoroughly; the PCC felt devalued and frustrated; and in practice real power continued to lie with the Vicar alone. An extended review led them to decide to separate the executive and the pastoral side of their work. First, they set up the sort of extended Standing Committee described in the next section, responsible to the PCC on all policy matters including finance, and responsible also for appointing a Pastoral Team. The latter was briefed to share in whatever ways became appropriate in the whole pastoral side of the Vicar's work, including preaching and leading worship, the leadership of house groups, and baptism and marriage preparation.

This pragmatic approach has two advantages. It divides up the work and helps make the best use of the gifts of busy people; and it helps point to the difference between the legal and constitutional authority of the Vicar, churchwardens and PCC, and the pastoral and spiritual authority, which technically lies with the same people but which has to be delegated to those who have the time and appropriate gifts for exercising it.

3. The management team

This can take a variety of forms: it may start as an enlarged standing committee or as an extension of the staff meeting, or (especially in larger churches) as a meeting of 'heads of departments'. Any of these can easily develop into some sort of eldership.

The enlarged standing committee

In one small country parish, the Vicar began by meeting regularly with his standing committee, co-opting a retired clergyman, a Reader, and one other. So far they have deliberately avoided giving the group or its members any official title, but in practice they are beginning to be seen by the church as an eldership, as they share together in the thinking and planning which formerly the Vicar did on his own.

In a terraced-housing parish in the north, the standing committee co-opted two deputy wardens and one other, so as to include all three Readers. They meet for one full evening a month, as well as for a brief time of prayer each week, to deal with formal business and also to give time to considering the whole church life – people, plans and priorities.

In many churches, a standing committee of five, extended perhaps to seven or eight, seems to be the right size to work together effectively as a team.[2] Because it has a recognized constitutional position in church life – in theory if not always in practice – the standing committee often proves a good starting point for a long-term planned move towards real shared leadership. Its members should already have the confidence of the congregation. The main problem is that they may not always have the right gifts for leadership.

The extended staff meeting

This typically includes Readers as well as churchwardens, and perhaps a deputy warden or other lay person with a specific area of responsibility (for example, youth work, visiting, or house groups). The 'staff' might include paid lay staff, as well as the ordained ministers, but many churches are happy to speak of an 'extended staff meeting' where the full-time staff is just one man!

One such group in a small northern city meets every week from 7.00 to 9.00 am. They find that evenings are impossible and the five 'workers' in the team of seven all work very locally. They describe their priorities as first, prayer, then people, policies and plans. Other groups alternate an early prayer breakfast with a full meeting once a fortnight in the evening or a Saturday morning. Many such groups make a point of drawing in their spouses on a regular basis to avoid the risk of creating tension in marriages, and also, where the team is mostly men, because so often their wives have a very great deal to contribute.

One church with a substantial civic role in a town centre has found it necessary to have both kinds of group. The extended staff meeting (two clergy, one NSM and three Readers) has a weekly prayer breakfast, and also a monthly pastoral planning meeting into which others with pastoral responsibility are being drawn. The regular standdding committee meets for necessary administrative business. Between them, all the necessary elements of the work are fully covered, and the lay leadership is used in the most effective way, without excessive over-loading of busy people.

The emphasis of the extended staff meeting lies in its sharing some of the work of the Minister; the emphasis of the extended standing committee generally seems to lie more in its relation to the Church Council. In practice, this distinction is seldom very clear-cut, perhaps especially in large churches. For example, in one church with almost 1,000 members, where the Church Council of thirty-five meets only six times a year, and all the work is done through a large number of sub-committees, the threads are held together by a 'Church Leaders Group', which meets twice a month, with an occasional day away together. This consists of five out of the nine paid staff, five church-wardens and deputy wardens, and two Readers. Six members of this team divide between them the oversight of more than thirty house groups, and one of them co-ordinates this part of their work. The Leaders' Group includes the whole standing committee, and operates as such where necessary. Its very wide-ranging function, as agreed by the Church Council, is to: (a) provide fellowship and support for paid members of staff; (b) monitor the day-to-day work and expenditure of the church; (c) consider important issues and report as necessary to the council. This is seen as including appointments of staff and of leaders in church organizations, and also planning parish weekends, teaching and preaching programmes, and missionary activity.

It is clear that here, as in many churches with a large full-time staff, there are two particular pressures. First, because the staff meet weekly, they have to put up with the fact that a number of matters are discussed twice over, both at the staff meeting and at the Church Leaders Group. Secondly, there is great pressure on the lay members of the Group in keeping up with the thinking and work of the staff team. It becomes virtually impossible for lay members in full-time work to take on any other major Christian responsibility outside their local church.

This sort of group is not only typical of large churches. At the other end of the scale a small back-street congregation of about fifty members made a first move in the same direction by appointing three deputy wardens 'to share the burden with the churchwardens' who at that stage were doing virtually every job in the church between them – secretary, treasurer, church-yard and buildings, as well as welcoming everybody at the church door. The Vicar now meets regularly with this team of five, and is drawing them gradually into a sense of shared responsibility with each other and with him for the whole life and work of the church. They meet together and share, pray and learn, and slowly take on more responsibility. As they are stretched, they grow, and in due course they could become an effective team.

The 'heads of departments' team

Another pattern common in large churches is what can best be called a 'heads of departments' team. Although in some cases it might have very much the same membership as the extended staff or standing committee, its reason for coming together is rather different.

Where there is a great volume of activity, and many lay members involved, it often seems essential for those with particular responsibilities to meet regularly in order to co-ordinate work and avoid confusion. Such a group often consists of the chairmen of the various sub-committees of the Church Council, together with one or more of the clergy, the church-wardens, or the Readers. In a less formal structure it might be the leaders of various working groups appointed by the Church Council or church meeting.

In one suburban church which has grown from 100 to 400 members in the last five years, seven lay people (including both churchwardens) meet once each month with the Vicar and Curate. Each has a particular responsibility, such as oversight of youth work or house groups, or chairing a PCC committee. In spite of the pressure on the time of busy people, they all see this meeting as an essential complement to the weekly staff meeting and the bi-monthly Church Council.

Another team of this kind emerged out of a small group which had at first been set up to share in the pastoral care of the whole congregation. In this case those appointed to this team by the Vicar and churchwardens very quickly found that they were gravitating into responsibility for specific parts of church life: one for young families and family services, one for the Sunday school team, and one into leading a large team involved with visiting the elderly. The danger here is always that if such a management team is too large in relation to the Church Council or meets too frequently, it can find itself very naturally reaching decisions, and so leaving the Church Council with virtually nothing to do except raise objections or to rubber-stamp the team's decisions, neither of which is satisfactory. It is essential that everyone understands that the team is no more than a co-ordinating group, with no authority of its own beyond what has been specifically given it, and that all its proposals should therefore come back to the Church Council as recommendations, not as decisions.

Another problem with a heads of department team is that most of its members by definition already have substantial responsibilities within the church, which they may be fulfilling extremely well. But they may not have either the time, the ability or the vision to take a wider view of the whole life and direction of the church. So the extended staff meeting or

standing committee is probably an easier and more natural way
forward towards corporate leadership.

4. The pastoral leadership (sometimes called eldership).
Any of the teams previously decribed can find themselves
moving outside their initial brief. As they grow in pastoral
responsibility their ability to share in the leadership grows as
well. A pastoral team, a team of house group leaders, a
consultative group or an extended staff meeting or standing
committee can all find that they are gradually coming to share
more and more in some of the responsibilities traditionally
exercised by the Minister on his own.

On the other hand, some churches which already have a
number of mature and able members may find that they can
set up a pastoral leadership team, and may indeed refer to it
as 'the eldership', without any transitional stages. Whatever
title the team is given – and there is a remarkable variety – the
key feature distinguishing this from the three other approaches
to shared leadership is the team's relationship with the Minister.

For example, in churches where deacons are traditionally
seen as very distinct from the Minister or Pastor, the emergence
of an eldership immediately enlarges the leadership from one
man to a team. Many Anglican churches with some sort of
eldership team explained that it felt like having a 'corporate
Vicar'. Others, perhaps wishing to retain a clear emphasis on
the continuing leadership role of the Vicar, described the team
as a corporate Curate.[3] Some recognized that, at least at first,
it was very much like a junior Curate with relatively little
experience, and a great deal to learn; in other cases the team
was clearly more like a senior Curate, perhaps virtually an
equal colleague, with a wide range of experience, but perhaps
still a lot to learn as well. Those which start like a junior Curate
can develop surprisingly quickly – and this growth can itself
become a source of tension.

The major emphasis of the work of such teams varies greatly.
In some cases it is on planning the teaching programme of the
church and on worship, in others on priorities and policies,
while in others it is people and pastoral care. For worship and
teaching, the team brings together differing skills and gifts and
a wider background of experience. The stimulus of working in
a team can improve what is available in both areas. Where
priorities and policies are concerned, ideas come with the

benefit of previous discussion in a small group, instead of the Minister bringing suggestions to the Church Council, and that larger body seldom having the time for thorough discussion. In the case of people and pastoral care, the team shares the load previously carried by one man, with the result that difficult situations are much more likely to receive proper attention and help.

The best way to indicate the variety of ways in which these teams work in practice is to summarize some of their own self-descriptions. In each case, details of the team and its method of meeting are given as a background.

1. A large northern parish: two clergy, two Readers (out of five), two ex-churchwardens, three other lay people; one long Saturday evening and one short Sunday evening each month.

'We meet to share our own needs and concerns personally – as well as those of people in the congregation; to grow together as a group, in worship and prayer; and to think through church policy and plans. This has made possible much better pastoral care for people with deep needs, and better decision-making by the Church Council. It has been an immense release for me, as Vicar, to share so many of the burdens over the last three years.'

2. A Baptist church on the south coast: two staff began meeting with four deacons in 1976; there are now four staff and eight elders meeting weekly (once a month with wives as well).

'Three of the elders have specific responsibilities – youth, visiting and oversight of the whole home-group work. Each is therefore concerned for between twenty and forty helpers, leaders and assistants. The others each have a link with three or four of the home groups. We have a monthly meeting with home-group leaders for prayer, planning and sharing. Each of our home groups has a list of people for whom it has a pastoral concern.'

3. A suburban parish in the south-east: a team of nine with quite a turnover in its first four years (one left for theological college, two moved because of work; but one retired and was then able to become almost a full-time worker); the team meets monthly, often beginning with a meal together.

'Three of the lay members head up teams of their own – one for hospital/sick visiting, one for all the youth helpers, one for the house group leaders. We all share concern for individual pastoral needs. Some of us also have responsibility for a geographical area, and the two or three house groups within that area. We are happy, at the moment, with what feels like an untidy, flexible, interim stage, and we're in no hurry to move on.'

4. An Assemblies of God church in the north: the Minister meets his four spare-time elders twice each month, and every Sunday to pray for half an hour before morning worship.

'Our main task is that each of us oversees five or six home-groups; with so many new Christians and young leaders, constant care here is essential. We also plan and review our Sunday worship and teaching, share in forward thinking, and pray and plan for the development of leadership in every area of our church life and work. We keep the whole church closely in touch with all our thinking.'

5. A small suburban parish: Vicar, Churchwarden, Reader and one other meet for an hour once a week, with a day away together three times a year.

'We pray for each other, for people and for plans; we do the preliminary thinking on all policy and pastoral matters coming up to the PCC – but never make decisions unless the Church Council specifically asks us to do so.'

6. A terrace-housing London parish: a team of ten, no title, meeting one evening a month; all the team have been on a deanery-based pastoral training course.

'At first we saw our work as "helping the Vicar", but two consecutive interregnums helped us grow; now we are sharing more and more in the whole "cure of souls". Each is involved in a different area of work – young families, Sunday School, youth, marriage preparation, hospital work, the bereaved. We share each other's concerns and find the mutual support of the team very helpful as we gradually take on more responsibility.'

7. A steel-works town in the north: two churches with two clergy and one full-time lay pastor, plus one Churchwarden and one pastoral elder from each church; meeting once a month for a meal on Sunday afternoon (plus wives occasionally) – the only relaxed time, due to shift-work and pressure on evenings.

'We try to assess what God is doing in people and in the church; we discuss pastoral issues and policy – we are still learning what it means to be leaders *and* servants of the whole church. In practice, two of us take the lead in the PCC, three of us have a major concern for home groups, and three of us are directly involved in pastoral work and drawing others into various visiting opportunities.'

8. A mill-town back-street parish: Vicar, two Church-wardens, two Readers and two others meet for one long evening each month.

'We began as a "pastoral standing committee" sharing ideas and plans before each PCC meeting. This grew into sharing pastoral burdens, and thinking through all our policies and practices at a deeper level – still bringing ideas at an early stage to the PCC where a PCC decision is appropriate. Between us we also oversee the work of eight house-group leaders and two teams of visitors.'

9. From other churches:

(i) 'At alternate meetings we draw in others involved in leadership; we meet home group leaders and the youth team about three times a year; we see the finance team, the visiting team, the missionary support committee and the 'Music in Worship' team once or twice a year; we also meet as necessary with those thinking towards ordination or other specific training.'

(ii) 'We see our house group leaders (all on the PCC) as the elders, and the rest of the PCC as the deacons.'

(iii) 'Our team grew out of the standing committee which was able to meet weekly to share and pray. Now ten of us have become a sort of corporate Vicar, some with responsibility for specific areas of the work. The key to growing into a real team is complete mutual trust and regular prayer together.'

(iv) 'The team has saved me from a number of misjudge-ments – both in choosing people for jobs and in helping those with particular relationship problems. Members of the team often know people at a much deeper level than I can, so they may be more able to unravel complicated situations.'

Finally, to quote the Vicars of one very large suburban church and one small village, both of whose lay teams seemed to be working extremely well:

'The team has a vital role both in consulting with the staff and in preparing ideas for the PCC. They ensure the staff keep in touch with views on a wide variety of subjects; they act as a support group for staff who are always under pressure; they frequently improve ideas first floated at the staff meeting – and sometimes squash them completely; they help us get the pace of change right. We always try to bring new ideas to the PCC in a provisional way, or with alternative options. The PCC must retain the ultimate authority; so it is clearly wrong to produce cut-and-dried plans for rubber-stamping. It works far better when we bring a well-discussed paper and full information. Sometimes it is then given back to the staff or the eldership for making a final decision or recommendation in the light of further discussion; somtimes it comes back again to the PCC. We could never have coped with the growth of the last few years without the increasing wisdom and insight of the team.'

'I now have a team who know everyone – they know the history, they understand the tension between the old village and newcomers from outside. Together we believe we are much more likely to discover the way God wants the church to go – in its worship, in the rest of its internal life, and in all its local involvement with individuals and with the community. It's not just that I was an outsider, or that I only had seven days in each week. The team has insights and gifts which I lacked, and by bringing all the gifts together, we can give the church the leadership it needs.'

When is a pastoral leadership an eldership?

The present picture is an untidy one, with many blurred edges. The word 'elder' and the more commonly used corporate title 'eldership' are used to describe a considerable variety of situations. The so-called elders vary greatly in calibre and maturity; their work as an eldership and their relationship with their Minister varies greatly too. None of this should be surprising. Given the deeply rooted tradition and expectation of one-man-ministry, the rediscovery of the early-church principle of corporate local leadership, and the search for the best way of applying that principle in a very different society and culture, is bound to be untidy.

In times of transition and growth, which create their own tensions, any attempt to lay down tidy definitions and standard patterns at too early a stage is almost bound to create extra difficulties. Of course, we need to know the direction in which we are moving, the direction in which the Holy Spirit seems to be moving the church. But before taking out the crystal ball and trying to see where the church might be in twenty years' time and what needs to be done to help it get there, it is essential to be realistic about the problems that are already emerging on the early stages of the journey.

9: Lessons of corporate leadership

It would be foolish to pretend that the one-man ministry can be replaced by a corporate form of leadership without running into problems. But if churches and individuals are aware of the sort of difficulties they are likely to face, they should find it easier either to avoid them or to deal with them constructively when they occur. The problems can be best considered under four main headings: problems in initiating any form of local team; problems in developing a local team; problems within a more or less established local team; problems in renewing established teams.

Problems in initiating a local team

Because one-man leadership has been in practice the normal situation in almost every denomination, and Ministers, church officers and congregations have been brought up to expect it and work within it, it is not surprising that the idea of corporate leadership often seems such a threat to those involved that they are prejudiced against it from the start.

1. Opposition from the Minister

Given this long tradition and expectation of clerical domination, many clergy are naturally reluctant to step out into the unknown territory of corporate leadership, especially if they have heard 'horror-stories' of what has happened elsewhere. But even so, this reluctance has several real foundations in legal, psychological and practical terms.

Some clergy feel that the very idea of shared leadership is logically impossible. In legal terms, the Minister has been called by the patrons or by the church, and has been put in charge at his institution and induction and given full authority and responsibility. If things go wrong, he knows that the buck stops with him, and all his training has assumed that he will have this sole authority. His relationship with church council, deacons and congregation is prescribed by the law or the Trust deeds and endorsed by tradition; any change is certain to affect this relationship, and can easily be felt as a threat to his personal position.

In psychological terms, the experience of generations has created attitudes of dependence which are highly persistent. As Anthony Russell says: 'The presence of a highly trained man whose role it is to promote the goals of the organisation, encourages those around him to leave matters entirely in his hands.'[1] Particularly where visible and measureable success is limited, some Ministers need to cling on to this position of total authority in which others are dependent upon their leadership in order to achieve a sense of personal significance. Some lack the security of knowing that they are loved and valued by God and by their friends for what they *are*, rather than for what they have achieved, and are therefore hesitant to launch out into uncharted waters where their status and their performance (or lack of it) may be questioned. Some, too, are by nature loners. Such people often have a clear vision and deep commitment, and want to get on with 'doing their own thing' to which they have been called, without the frustrations (as they see it) of having to share every stage of the process with others. They do not want to be held back from pursuing their own vision by yet another committee.

More importantly, at the practical level, the Minister may be reluctant to share his leadership role for one of two opposite reasons: the lay team may not be good enough to do the job properly, or they may be so good at it that they show up his own inadequacies. In the first case, it is he who has the professional ability based on training and practical experience. It is often said that few people think it sensible to seek medical, legal or investment advice from a spare-time, untrained, non-accredited amateur, particularly where the services of a trained professional are available at no cost! Why should the church be different?

Moreover, the first steps a Minister takes in delegating responsibility all too often end up in failure: the job is not done, or not done properly; the pastoral needs are not met –

indeed sometimes the situation is made worse; and it would clearly have been far better to have done it himself in the first place! It is obviously important to recognize that the Minister will normally have more theological insight and more pastoral experience than his lay leaders simply because he has been trained, he has read more widely and he has been doing for some years on a full-time basis what they may just be learning to do in their spare time. 'A full-time Minister has more understanding of the issues: it is mock-modesty to pretend that he is in the same position as everybody else.'[2] 'It is difficult to make equality real,' wrote a Baptist Minister, 'either in our own minds or in those of the congregation, when I am the one working at the job full-time; and especially when preaching and teaching happens to be my gift and not conspicuously the gift of my fellow-elders'. Shared leadership has to recognize reality.

At the opposite extreme, however, a new young Minister coming to his first church may find himself confronted with a group of lay leaders with considerable secular experience in different professional capacities, the pastoral wisdom which comes from greater age, and considerable knowledge of their church members. They will have kept the show going since the previous Minister left, and some of them may have greater natural ability than he has in one or more of the tasks which are traditionally seen as belonging particularly to the Minister. One or more of them may clearly be at least as good a preacher, pastor, chairman or leader of worship. All this can be very threatening.

These problems are real, but most of them can be avoided if there is a clear understanding of what is meant by shared leadership in this particular situation; if there is a common desire to search for the right leadership structure to make the church more effective.

The legal position of the Minister obviously cannot be undermined in any way by setting up a lay team, unless he deliberately chooses to ignore it; so it is essential that the role of the team and their relationship with the Minister, however informal, is thoroughly clarified and agreed.

The psychological problem is more difficult. Clergy of all denominations who want to act as 'pope in their own parish' will inevitably retain a dominant role over whatever lay leadership they allow to emerge. This may not always be a bad thing.

In many areas, particularly where an attitude of dependence is strongly entrenched in the congregation, lay leadership will develop best within the security of strong leadership from the Minister. For this he must himself have a long-term vision for shared leadership, but be content to start where people are and help them grow, to see more in them than is visible on the surface, to stretch them, encourage them, train them and stay with them until they can become a real team of colleagues. If for psychological reasons the Minister cannot enter into this vision, there is little that can be done except to pray that his whole approach will change, and to work towards giving him a sense of security and self-esteem that does not depend upon his status and authority.

Fears at the more practical level usually spring from false expectations. Where the lay leaders have a limited capacity it is clearly important not to ask more of them than they can give, and not to describe as 'elders' those who do not yet really match up to that title. On the other hand, where there is real ability in the team, the Minister has the privilege of being their leader, and therefore also their servant. He has the task of guiding, and perhaps restraining, the use and development of their gifts, which can be even more demanding than trying to do everything on his own. Far from downgrading his position, responsibilities and rôle, the establishment of a team enhances and enriches them.

The problem is that at present very few clergy receive any training – either in college or subsequently – in this vital area of team development. The unknown is often seen as a threat (as in the famous Guinness advertisement 'I don't like it, because I've never tried it') and not only by the clergy. Problems are just as likely to emerge from members of the congregation.

2. Opposition from church officers and Church Council

The emergence of a leadership team can also be felt as a threat by the elected Church Council, church wardens or deacons, with their traditional and official responsibilities. As with the clergy, there may be legal, psychological and practical grounds for such feelings.

It is clearly important not to undermine the legal position of councils and officers duly elected by the congregation. It is therefore essential that they all understand what sort of leadership team is emerging or being discussed, and exactly how it will relate to them, and that they approve. At every stage it should be made clear that their position is not being challenged.

At the psychological level, there are still churchwardens, church secretaries and deacons who value highly their position and the public status it gives them, and who see the team as a personal threat. Here, too, it may be necessary to work patiently through a long period of preparation and education, in order to make it clear that the proposed development neither challenges their position nor condemns the way they have been doing their work. However, this underlines the desirability of including the leading church officers within the team wherever possible.

At the practical level, concern arises mainly in two areas. There is a very proper fear that the duly elected or appointed representatives of the congregation might be bypassed by a small, possibly self-perpetuating elite who are not accountable to anyone, and that this might cause division in the church. Secondly, there is the fear of a further level of bureaucracy, with an extra tier inserted between the clergy and the church officers. Both these fears can be proved groundless if the team is set up with a proper structure for appointment, reporting and accountability, and especially if it is seen to function, within the existing organization, either as an 'extension' of the Minister and staff or as an equivalent of a pastoral standing-committee.

When the team is formed mainly from those who already hold recognized positions in the church this problem hardly occurs, except when the team grows so large that it comes to dominate the Church Council or deacons' meeting. One 'extended staff' team in Lichfield grew to fifteen in number, including two clergy, two churchwardens and four deputies, four Readers and two Sunday school superintendents. They gradually discovered that they were pursuing policy dicussions to such lengths at their regular monthly meetings that there was little left for the Church Council to do, and this was seen as unsatisfactory by everyone. This 'extended staff', which has recently grown even larger, now meets only three times a year, and purely for consultation, while the clergy meet with two non-stipendiary ministers and two of the Readers every other week as a central 'think-tank' and advisory group.

In a very different type of church, a group of elders in Sidcup,

Kent, grew steadily from six to thirteen, and in a similar way found they had almost eliminated the need for a Church Council. Their solution was to identify six main areas of responsibility, to allocate each to one member of the team, and then ensure that each area was the main item on the Church Council agenda once a year. The eldership as such was dissolved by agreement, although not without some pain, and replaced by a small informal Vicar's Advisory Group of four, which included two of the 'Heads of Departments'. The Church Council was then clearly left as the main forum for discussion, as well as decision, on all major issues.

In theory, it is possible for a large leadership team actually to replace the Church Council; or for the whole Council to be seen as the leadership. Indeed, this can work in practice, in exceptional circumstances. For example, one rapidly growing Anglican church in Singapore has a Church Council of nine, which meets with the two clergy for three or four hours every Saturday afternoon! At least one church in England is working on the same lines. After some months of teaching and study, they decided that their PCC of twelve members should be the eldership. They therefore agreed a 'job description' for eldership which included a commitment to two evenings each month and to sharing in the pastoral care of church members. This was circulated well before the next Annual Meeting. This has so far worked well, although some of those elected have found they could not give the necessary time and others lacked the gifts to share fully in the pastoral work. Each year some of the PCC have retired, moved away or left for other reasons, and have been replaced. The frequency of their meetings ensures that business usually takes less time than prayer and worship, study and teaching, and the regular discussion of plans and policies means that there is a much wider sense of involvement, and better communication with the whole membership.

Most Church Councils in England seem to be between twenty and twenty-five in number, and at that size it is just not possible to achieve the degree of closeness necessary to function as a pastoral leadership team. Most of them also meet too infrequently for such work, and in practice most of them are elected with a rather different purpose in mind. In many, there is a deliberate attempt to have some degree of representation – of age groups, of areas of church life, and indeed geographically. Some members are elected for their special skills to do with finance or property, which is all quite different from the business of pastoral leadership.

An Anglican Church Council has a very substantial job description. It is to 'consult together on matters of concern in the parish . . . to co-operate with the incumbent in promoting the whole mission of the church – pastoral, evangelistic, social and ecumenical'. Obviously much of this can best be done if there is an efficient system of sub-committees, and particularly if the administration of finance and property are in competent hands. Even so, there is in practice an immense load of non-pastoral matters which swamp the agenda of even the best-run Church Councils. So even if they have the right sort of membership to deal properly with matters of pastoral concern, they are unlikely to have the time. There is a real gap for some kind of pastoral leadership team as part of the structure.

Problems in this area can easily be made worse if the Minister or the team are excessively enthusiastic, and so create exaggerated expectations. In one big parish which took the establishment of a team very seriously, with widespread involvement over two years in thinking through both the theological principles and their practical application, the cry was later heard, 'But what does this eldership actually *do?*' It takes time for the value of a team to be recognized. More seriously, excessive enthusiasm can lead to 'jumping on the bandwagon' without sufficient preparation, without properly working out the most appropriate way ahead for the local situation, and without the convinced support of the established officers of the church.

3. Opposition from the congregation

There may also be considerable suspicion of any suggestion of corporate leadership among the congregation as a whole. In places where traditional expectations are very strong, there is often a deeply rooted reluctance to contemplate change of any kind. This is particularly common where numbers are declining, and it may require some years of patient and persistent education, or else the shock treatment of not being able to replace a retiring Minister, to change attitudes.

However, there can also be opposition in churches where there is considerable life and activity. 'Why change things when everything is going so well?' Here too education is necessary, at the level which a good stewardship campaign or the sort of systematic review procedure known as a Parish Audit can produce if the whole congregation is involved. It may then become clear to everyone that the Minister is grossly over-worked; that many pastoral needs are not being met; and that the congregation is maintaining its position simply because of new members transferring in from elsewhere.[3]

Even where there are many active lay-run church organiz-ations, there may be a fear of an élite of some kind being imposed over their heads. This fear may be based on hearsay, on stories of trouble in other congregations. In may be particu-larly acute if the obvious potential members of the leadership team are in any way 'apart' from the rest of the congregation. It is very natural for them to be among the more articulate members; often they will be those who are 'upwardly socially mobile'. If this means that they have also moved away from the immediate neighbourhood, or are in any other way 'distanced' from the majority of the congregation, such fear is very understandable. There may too be an element of jealousy, a willingness to accept the authority of the Minister, 'because he's different, and because he's paid for it; but no one wants x or y telling us what to do – they're no different from us anyway'. There is also a natural resistance to the possibility of a 'Vicar's clique'.

In some denominations there is a deep sense of the ultimate constitutional authority of the Church Meeting. The Church Meeting hires and fires the Minister, elects the deacons, and woe betide anyone who tries to alter the constitution or the Trust Deed! They expect Minister and deacons to go on doing their traditional tasks, but the idea of an eldership from within their own membership challenges the authority of the whole body, particularly if they have heard stories of authoritarian behaviour by newly-appointed elders elsewhere.

Finally, congregational opposition is often based very simply and reasonably on fear of gossip. People are accustomed, at least in theory, to sharing their burdens with their Minister, on a basis of total confidentiality. 'Will this still be possible if we set up a team? Or will our inner secrets be all round the congregation in a week?' This is a real problem, but it is in fact already a problem wherever there are people other than the Minister involved in any real way in pastoral care. This under-lines the importance of choosing for the team people who have sufficient wisdom and maturity not to be gossips. Some pastoral teams work on the basis that individual problems are only ever mentioned anonymously. This may work well in large congregations, where other team members are unlikely to recognize the situation being described. Others find that this makes it more difficult to pray, and to find the right way of helping – in which case it is essential to have asked the individual concerned whether the problem may be shared with the Minister, or with the team, on a confidential basis.

This all points to the need for the whole congregation to be involved at the earliest possible stage in the whole preparatory process. They need to understand what sort of a leadership team is being proposed, and why it is thought to be necessary. They need to feel that their contribution to the discussion has been heard, and that the decision to go ahead is theirs. It is essential that they are involved in some way in the selection and appointment of the team, and not just expected to give their approval to a list of names. They must feel that the list is composed of people in whom they have confidence.

Three conclusions emerge from this discussion of relationships between the team and the Minister, the Church Council and church officers, and the congregation. First, it is essential not to go too fast, nor to move too far ahead of the point people have reached in their understanding of church and ministry; to take time to educate, to learn from the experience of others, and to work out together what is the right and appropriate way forward. Secondly, it is necessary for roles and relationships to be clarified from the beginning, and for these to be kept carefully under review, bearing in mind that the team itself, and its individual members, will be developing in character and maturity as a result of working together. Thirdly, it is vital to establish and retain total mutual trust within the team; and this requires time. These problems of clarity of role and of time are very much at the heart of the difficulties experienced as teams begin to develop.

Problems in developing a local team

Mutual trust within the team is essential for effective team work, but remarkably difficult to achieve and then maintain. The first enemy is the sheer pressure of time, but the time problem is always made even worse if there is no agreed understanding on the nature and function of the team. This is important at the stage of setting up a team, but vital as the team settles in to its work. Often the character and capacity of the team develops and deepens from the point at which it began, and sometimes its function changes as well.

1. The need for clarity

If there is no clear understanding of the team's precise nature and function there will often be duplication of effort and discussion. This makes the time-problem worse, and leads to frustration and misunderstandings within the team, between individuals and between groups in the church. For this reason it is desirable that the team not only conducts a regular internal review, probably on an annual basis, of what it is actually doing and trying to do, but also that it reports equally regularly to the Church Council, deacons, or annual Church Meeting.

It may well be helpful if an outside consultant can be brought in to help the team ask itself the right questions and face up to difficult issues, personality clashes, or other emerging problems at as early a stage as possible, as well as to add the benefit of experience of what is happening in such teams elsewhere. The consultant can help the team identify significant changes in its own development as a team, which it may be unwilling or unable to recognize or acknowledge. He may be able to help deal with difficult situations; for example, when it is necessary to persuade someone to retire from the team, or to agree on how to bring new members into it, or to deal with potential conflict or division at an early stage.

The team itself, or the Minister, or even the congregation may have had exaggerated expectations of what it was expected to achieve. It may have started on a wrong footing, and it may be necessary to close it down completely and pause for a time before making a fresh start. It may have become distanced from the congregation without realising it. It may have become bogged down by insisting on unanimity in its decisions. In some cases the Minister himself may be the problem; in others he may be alone in seeing the problem but feel unwilling or unable to reassert his authority over the team to impose a solution. In all these situations, where considerable pain may be involved, an outside consultant who is already known and whose judgement is respected by the team can be an immense help. He may indeed often be the answer to Robert Burns' prayer:

> *Oh would some Power the giftie gie us*
> *To see ourselves as others see us!*
> *It would from many a blunder free us*
> *And foolish notion.*

It has been noted that many teams have simply 'emerged' at a very informal level in different ways. As soon as they begin to play a significant part in the life of the congregation, their role needs to be defined, and the discipline of making an annual report to the Church Council or being questioned by a consultant, can be a great help in ensuring that this is done properly. In many situations, confusion could have been avoided if the team had had clear terms of reference and if these were kept under regular review. It then becomes easier to discuss the setting of goals, both for the team and the church, to separate tactics from strategy and to arrange for proper mutual support and care for members of the team. This last item is particularly important for those under pressure from their secular work or their family commitments. When the nature and the purpose of the team is clear, it is easier to tackle the almost universal problem of time.

2. The pressure of time.
Many clergy expressed serious concern about the pressure put on their emerging lay leadership, and indeed this was often seen as the main barrier to the deeper development of the team's growth and usefulness. Again and again, comments like this were made by Ministers:

'I hardly dare ask those with young families or big responsibilities in their secular work to take on anything more – in fact, some of them really ought to reduce their church commitments . . . So many barely have time to do their present church job thoroughly. How can they possibly give the extra time necessary for sharing in overall policy and planning?'

' . . . To become a real team we must spend more time together; but there are just not enough hours in the week.'

' . . . It was leading to serious stress in one or two families and marriages, so we disbanded the team.'

' . . . Some of the team were away so often that we never developed a real sense of unity and common purpose.'

There is no magic answer to the problem, but obviously it is important to be realistic, rather than attempt the impossbile.

You can only start with whoever is available, and within the constraints of their existing commitments. It may be necessary to question those commitments; or to question the proliferation of 'church meetings' which those with leadership responsibilities are expect to attend. It is almost certainly necessary to delegate work. Deputy wardens can assist and relieve churchwardens, if the churchwardens are to be part of an eldership team. Another house group leader must be found, if one of them is to be freed to oversee all the house groups. If busy people are to be set free to share in leadership, others must be drawn in to help. The overload of the few, which is such a common complaint, can only be solved by spreading their work among others. It is easy to think that no-one else could possibly take on any more. If that is really the case, if a search through the membership list reveals no-one with potential for taking on extra work, then possibly the whole range of church activities needs to be scrutinized. But almost always there are people with potential. Many of them may take time to draw in, and they may need to work alongside someone for a period of training, which is often the best way of learning a new job anyway.

Imaginative use must also be made of all those who do have time available. Churches are sometimes more guilty of 'ageism' (ignoring the experience, wisdom and availability of older people) than of the racism or sexism with which they are more frequently charged! Some women with grown-up families drift back into work because they have nothing else to do! An increasing number of people are now taking early retirement. Many disabled people have gifts that can be developed and used, and often have time on their hands. Today no less than in New Testament times, there are widows (1 Tim. 5: 9–10) whose gifts are often underused. In many places, with suitable encouragement and support and proper planning, such people can take on much of the pastoral care of the sick, the bereaved and those in hospital (travel expenses might need to be paid). Some of them may also be able to help significantly with other regular visiting, or assist in preparation for marriage, baptism or confirmation.

One of the first tasks of a new eldership team, perhaps even before it is formed, is to assess its own workload and see what needs to be delegated if the members of the team are to have the time necessary for their work together as elders.

Alongside the frequent complaints that pressure of time was the chief problem in developing an eldership team came the insistence that time together as a team was vital. Examples have already been quoted to show how different teams have tackled this, and the solution must obviously vary according to the commitments of those involved. But experience suggests that some sort of meeting on a weekly basis is necessary if the team is really to grow together into the closeness and mutual trust required for effective work and for overcoming potential problems. The pattern most frequently favoured is a fortnightly meeting (usually for a full evening or a Saturday morning, often beginning with a meal together) for prayer and all the rest of the eldership business, preferably with some sort of regular programme. There would also be a shorter gathering for prayer in the alternate weeks, often for a prayer-breakfast or before (or after) church service on a Sunday.

This is obviously very demanding. It may make it impossible for some people to join the team, and in some places it may simply not be possible to meet with this regularity. If that is really the case, then extra precautions will be needed to avoid the other problems of confusion, misunderstanding and division. Many churches have found it an immense help if the team can have an 'away-day' together, or even half a day two or three times a year. Some have greatly valued an occasional weekend or holiday together, while others have decided to ease the pressure by insisting that each member of the team takes a full year off, on a regular basis. Others allow for a regular 'sabbatical' so that team members in turn can take three months 'off duty', during which time they are not expected to attend a single church meeting!

At a very practical level, some teams have vastly reduced the proliferation of meetings by deliberately planning them into a regular programme. One team meets every fortnight, say twenty-five times a year. Three of these evenings are set aside to meet with the house group leaders, three for the standing committee, two for the youth team, and one each for missionary supporters, the finance team, and those considering a call to full-time service. Far from being 'just another piece of bureaucracy', a planned programme like this can ensure that every part of church life is properly considered at the pastoral level, and out of such a programme, material can be fed to the

Church Council, deacons, or church meeting in a way that will make it easier for them to reach right decisions.

It does need to be said, however, that real growth in the church is going to require costly sacrifices of time, as well as money. It may be necessary for some people to make a decision between promotion to a more demanding secular job and deeper involvement in the life of the church. For others, it may mean the wider choice between a full-time and a part-time job, or between a part-time job and making their whole time available for the church. They may need considerable pastoral help in making such a decision. This applies particularly to the increasing number of self-employed, to those whose long-term job security is uncertain, and to those whose secular work seems to be making ever-increasing demands on their time and energy.

In this context it is necessary to face up to the charge that the whole business of developing lay leadership is simply 'clericalizing the laity' and reinforcing the wholly false impression that to be a serious Christian it is necessary to be fully committed to church-based (and often to church-building-based) activities, thus apparently ignoring the priority of ministry in and to the world. The fact is that the fall in numbers in full-time clergy in the last twenty years has not been matched by a similar fall in the number of congregations they are required to serve; many more lay people are therefore already needed simply to keep the machinery of the church going.

But much more important than this, the development of a local leadership team, with varied gifts, is essential to the proper outward mobilization of the whole lay membership. In the short term this will certainly mean that a small number will have to concentrate on sharing in building up the inner life of the church. As a result, they themselves will have *less* time and energy to contribute as Christians in the world; but this has to be accepted, in the long-term interests of the greater effectiveness of the whole body in both church and world. Shared ministry, in the fullest sense, can only become a reality if there is shared leadership, and shared leadership requires time.

It requires time from the clergy, as well as from the lay leaders involved. Yves Congar, one of the early prophets of lay ministry, wrote: 'The development of Christian activity among lay people has added heavy burdens to the priestly ministry . . . it has opened up new aspects of his role, as

educator and spiritual trainer, and has enlarged and complicated his duties to a remarkable degree.'[4] Building a lay team
from scratch is indeed hard work: harder, at first, than doing
everything on one's own. Perhaps this is why many are
unwilling to try, and why others have failed. It is hard work,
and continuing hard work, because an emerging and developing
team needs continuing care and attention. The ordinary business of supervision and delegation takes time, and inevitably
more time is required for planning, for discussion, for prayer,
and for reporting back. There is however an even deeper
problem. The greater the ability of team members, the more
the scope for division; and division is not only painful to all
those involved, but also immensely time-consuming.

Problems within an established team

No type of team seems to be immune from this problem of
division, and indeed, both the New Testament and ordinary
common sense should warn us that division is to be expected.
In practical terms, misunderstanding and confusion are
commonest when people are under pressure, when roles and
relationships are new, and when the security of long experience
is missing.

1. New Testament warnings

There are plenty of warnings about division in the New Testament. The team who had the unique privilege of personal
tuition from Jesus were not immune from it. No effort is made
to conceal the fact that, as well as often failing to understand
Jesus and deserting him under pressure, they were as self-
centred, jealous, argumentative and concerned for their own
status as we are. Division and disunity within the church was
a problem from the earliest days.

Divisions can arise from disagreements on doctrine. Jesus
warned the church to be on its guard against false prophets
(Mt. 7: 15) 'who will deceive many people . . . who will
perform great signs and miracles, to deceive even the elect'
(Mt. 24: 11, 24). Peter, John, Jude and Paul echo the same
warning against division, which can only occur if there is
division in the leadership. 'There will be false teachers among
you . . . introducing destructive heresies, even denying the
sovereign Lord who bought them' (2 Pet. 2: 1); 'I am writing

about those who are trying to lead you astray' (1 Jn. 2: 26); ' . . . many false prophets, who have gone out into the world' (1 Jn. 4: 1) ' . . . deceivers, who do not acknowledge Jesus Christ as coming in the flesh' (2 Jn. 7); 'Certain men . . . have secretly slipped in among you . . . who deny Jesus Christ our only Sovereign and Lord . . . These are the men who divide you, who follow mere natural instincts and do not have the Spirit' (Jude 4, 19).

Division is particularly common on charismatic issues. In *Fullness and Freedom*, his commentary on Colossians, Dick Lucas suggests that that whole letter is a plea for Christian unity – a plea that became necessary because of false teachers, 'leaders arising within the Christian communities, teaching with conviction a spirituality that owed more to the spirit of the age than to the teaching of Christ!' So Paul warned the church in Corinth about the 'super-apostles who were in fact false apostles' (2 Cor. 11: 5, 13); so he warned the church in Rome to 'watch out for those who cause divisions' (Rom. 16: 17); and he warned the elders of Ephesus, 'savage wolves will come in among you . . . even from your own number men will arise and distort the truth in order to draw the disciples after them' (Acts 20: 29f). They might even use Paul's own teaching as a lever for causing division, says Peter: 'Paul's letters contain some things hard to understand, which ignorant and unstable people distort, as they do the other scriptures, to their own destruction' (2 Pet. 3:16). Christian maturity is clearly essential.

Division can also focus on matters of personality. Paul was horrified to discover that at Corinth some were claiming to follow Apollos, some Peter, some himself, while some (the 'super-spiritual') were saying, 'We follow Christ' (1 Cor. 1:10–12). But human nature is very corruptible. It is easy to think of ourselves more highly than we ought to think (Rom. 12:5). It is not unknown for church leaders to be at loggerheads with each other, like Diotrephes, 'who loves to be first, and will have nothing to do with us . . . refuses to welcome the brothers . . . stops those who want to do so and puts them out of the church' (3 John 9–10). Paul and Barnabas disagreed sharply over whether or not Mark should go with them on their next journey, after he had apparently let them down on their previous expedition (Acts 15:37–40). In this case, their solution was to part company and go in different directions, but this is seldom desirable if there is a division in the leadership of the local church.

2. Practical experience

Human nature being what it is, division within the team can in practice arise out of a whole range of what may outwardly appear to be relatively trivial issues, such as the length of sermons, the language and style of worship, and the use of modern music, but even these may only be surface symptoms of deeper problems. These seem to focus in three areas, which may be linked together in some places: personality conflict, the pace of charismatic renewal, and the role of women in the team.

Conflict of personality

There can be division between Minister and team, within the team, or between one member and the rest of the team. Whatever the immediate cause, the background is usually that one person, like Diotrephes, 'loves to be first'. The clash may start during a vacancy or interregnum, the team as a whole may have become used to working together in a particular way, which the new Minister cannot accept, because he feels that his own position is threatened by it. Or one of the team may have developed an area of personal authority which he is reluctant to let go.

Conflict can emerge at any time. 'I had a dominant, articulate, assertive Reader, who had too many ideas for the rest of the team to cope with'; 'One of the team clearly wanted to be "head prefect" – with the benefit of hindsight he should never have been appointed'; 'One of the churchwardens regularly vetoed ideas he disagreed with, even threatening to call in the Bishop'; 'A Reader who was a good preacher wanted to preach every Sunday'; 'One member claimed to be *the* authority on counselling and tried to dictate to the rest of us'; ' . . . made the eldership a power-base for promoting his own pet ideas'; ' . . . vetoed more than one possible new member of the team because he knew they disagreed with him on certain issues'; ' . . . insisted on every decision he didn't like being referred to the Church Meeting'.

Problems linked with the charismatic renewal movement

There seems to be particular scope for disagreement when some of the church or the eldership (indeed even when all of them) become involved in charismatic renewal. It is a bitter irony that the movement which in many places has brought such blessing, joy, healing, new life and growth should also often be connected with division and schism in the church. This division is not just between those who are in favour of charismatic renewal and those who are against it. It also occurs within groups wholly committed to the principle of renewal. There can be division over the public use of tongues and of prophecy, or over the relationship between ordinary pastoral counselling and the ministry of deliverance and healing. Some of the eldership may want to move further and faster than others, or than Minister, deacons or Church Council feel is right, in new directions.

Sometimes these divisions seem to arise spontaneously, but often there is a link with an outside source. David Watson described what happened at St Michael-le-Belfry in York: 'a small group . . . were putting themselves under the authority of the leaders of (another) fellowship . . . apparently looking for a much stronger authority structure, involving more rigid discipling, shepherding and submission . . . advocating a different aspect of spirituality which had all the dangers of becoming a super-spirituality'[5]. Many churches have been through similar experiences, often involving much personal pain, and sometimes leading to one group being pushed out, or deciding to march out, and joining a neighbouring house church or starting up on their own. Such fragmentation can on rare occasions lead to there being two growing churches instead of only one before, but bitterness is seldom if ever a good foundation, and once the pattern of schism has been established, it tends to continue. Groups which have split away from their home church tend to split again whenever there is any major disagreement, instead of working through it to reach a common mind.

Conflict on the role of women in leadership

It may seem odd to identify this above all other doctrinal matters; but in fact it is a very common cause of division. There are deeply held views in pentecostal/charismatic circles, among other evangelicals, and also among those who start from a more Catholic position.

It becomes a particular problem where corporate leadership is emerging, for at least two reasons. First, almost no one thinks it odd for women to be involved in a pastoral team, whether based on visiting, or on house groups. Indeed, it is natural for a woman to be the leader of many such pastoral teams. What happens when the pastoral team is in the process of growing into a leadership team or eldership? A few Anglican churches are still reluctant to accept women as churchwardens or Readers, but this hesitation grows sharper and is felt in more churches when the extended staff team begins to become an eldership. In other denominations the pattern is varied. To make matters even more complicated, the charismatic renewal movement seems to have hardened people's attitudes in some places as they begin to take Scripture more literally, and to have softened their views elsewhere as an emphasis on freedom in the Spirit begins to challenge their traditional understanding of masculine superiority.[6]

Secondly, there is the specific and very sensitive problem arising from the position of the Minister's wife. In many churches, long before shared leadership emerges, the Minister's closest colleague, confidante, and counsellor is very naturally his wife. Her exclusion from an eldership group can cause particular pain in such situations. David Watson and his wife Anne experienced this in York, as he describes in a way many others would echo: 'The practical implications were painful for her. Up to this point Anne and I together had been the effective leaders of the work, as we tried to discern God's guidance for each new stage of development. Now . . . Anne was excluded from the leadership group'.[7] Some years later, the decision to bring three women into the eldership team was the last straw, which led to a small group breaking away from St Michael-le-Belfry, causing great pain and sorrow all round.

3. Resolving conflict
The sort of divisions described above are clearly contrary to the command and will of Christ. They greatly hinder the work and witness of the church, they are deeply painful for those involved, and they consume a vast amount of time and mental and spiritual energy, which could far better be spent in other directions. But how can division be avoided, and if it occurs, how can it best be healed? Five positive approaches can be identified, and all of them are usually necessary!

Recognize that some conflict is natural
It is essential first to recognize the potential for conflict in any living, growing organism. Adolescence is itself a time of considerable internal conflict, and most shared leadership teams

are in the adolescent stage of growth. As someone once said, 'growth involves tension: the only place of total rest and peace is the graveyard'. Conflict is equally natural within the leadership team, and indeed, it has been suggested that in teams (as in marriages) where there is no conflict at all, 'either the team do not know each other very well or they do not interact very much'. We must expect to face disagreements within the team at first, but we must be committed to finding a way through that disagreement, into a unity of purpose and aim which may well be stronger as a result of the stress which it has been through!

Identify the real cause of the conflict

The value has already been mentioned of using an outside consultant who is already known to the team, and is trusted by them. It is interesting to note that a considerable number of Baptist churches have recently begun to find for themselves just such a person, not solely to help them tackle this specific problem but because they see the need for an external resource for a variety of purposes, of which conflict therapy could be one.

In the Church of England the same sort of help should in theory be available through archdeacons and rural deans as they increasingly begin to share the pastoral oversight of the Bishop. In practice, this seldom works, because these men are usually under such pressure themselves already that they cannot give the time to get sufficiently involved. Some churches find the necessary external resources through other, less formal networks, but most have to battle through the problems on their own. There is a real need for a 'massive provision of in-service support groups, personal growth groups, and the availability of independent consultants backed by encouragement from above'.[8] Whether outside help is available or not, it is essential to identify the real problem, and to disentangle it from the confused mess of misunderstanding and growing distrust which is so often present.

Recognize that right attitudes are essential

Division is almost always associated with wrong attitudes. Shared leadership seems to bring out the worst in us, such as pride, jealousy, envy, malice. And there is an enemy, eager to capitalize upon human weakness in order to undermine the essential foundations of total mutual trust, forgiveness and humility. Jesus challenged the disciples with his own example: 'If I, your Lord and Teacher, have washed your feet, you also should wash one another's feet' (Jn. 13:14). Paul echoes this concern again and again; for example: 'Do nothing out of selfish ambition, but in humility consider others better than yourselves' (Phil. 2:3); 'Be humble and gentle, be patient, bearing with one another in love' (Eph. 4:2). It is desperately easy to forget the simple things like respecting each other, praying for each other, sharing each other's joys and pains, listening to each other, valuing each other as people even while disagreeing with their opinions, and above all learning to forgive each other, learning what Jesus means by reconciliation. 'If you remember that your brother has something against you, leave your gift there at the altar. First go and be reconciled to your brother; then come and offer your gift' (Mt. 5:23–24). This is far more than a readiness to forgive those who have offended us. It is a commitment to ask for forgiveness from those whom we have offended. Dare we ask, 'My brother, have I said or done anything that has hurt you?' It is never easy, but it may be vital.

Recognize the need for varied gifts
Humility means recognizing and valuing the gifts of other members of the team, rather than thinking we know it all because we have been ordained, or have completed a training course, or have been chosen and commissioned by the church as a pastoral elder. We need to recognize that God has chosen to give varied gifts to the church leadership, and that all of them are necessary if his purposes are to be fulfilled.

The lists of gifts in Romans chapter 12 and 1 Corinthians chapter 12 are all 'for the common good'. More specifically, the different leadership gifts of Ephesians 4:11 are clearly set in the context of unity. The purpose for which God has given the varied gifts is the effective ministry, the unity and the maturity of the body (4:12–13). The background within which they are given is the unity of the Holy Spirit (4:3) which we are to strive and struggle to preserve. We should not expect unity to come easily! Its basis, as Paul sets it out here, must be both unity of love and unity of doctrine. We are to be humble, gentle, bearing with one another in love (4:2), and we are to recognize that there is one body, one Spirit, one Lord, one faith, one baptism, one God and father of all (4:4–6).

In any human conflict, we need to remember that what unites us is vastly stronger and more important than what divides us. How then do we set about reaching a common mind?

Establish an agreed decision-making procedure
It is obviously desirable for this to be done at an early stage in the life of the team, certainly before any division has arisen. It is equally desirable to keep it under periodic review, since what is appropriate in the early stages may become less so later on. It is also useful to note that the procedure may need to vary. If the Minister disagrees with most or all of the rest of the team the situation is very different from when the team is itself divided.

The simplest answer is to recognize that the Minister has the final say – and there are many clergy who insist on this! If a man can really say, 'I make the decisions even if the whole team disagrees with me', it is usually a sign that something is deeply wrong, either with him, or in the team. In the Church of England the Minister is technically bound to win. In other denominations, it may well be that the Minister has to leave. Both situations are deeply unsatisfactory, not least because the 'winner' may well not be right!

Some teams have insisted on unanimity, and this too carries obvious risks. It may lead to interminable delays, and it can produce moral blackmail on the one individual who disagrees with the rest: 'The whole life of the church is held up because *you* won't agree'. Modified unanimity, on the lines of the majority vote in a jury, is therefore preferable. Every member of the team agrees in advance that if they alone are opposed to the others, they will either happily go along with them or else withdraw.

The only other alternative is the straightforward majority vote, which few people seem to like. In the first place, everyone knows that minorities are often right! Secondly, if the minority actually represent a substantial body of opinion in the church, there is unlikely to be really worthwhile support for going ahead on the basis of the majority recommendation. Many people, when asked how they reached their decisions, spoke as if there was a fourth way: 'We wait for a real consensus'; 'We don't move until we all feel it is right'. But in practice 'waiting for consensus' normally means that the majority have to wait for the minority to change their minds, and therefore that the minority have won, which is exactly the same as insisting on unanimity, except that it may avoid the formality of a vote. And it leaves the same moral pressure on the minority, to give up their 'narrow-minded obstruction'.

It is certainly useful to have an agreed framework in the background to cope with situations where disagreements have become deeply entrenched. If everyone has agreed on the Minister having the final word, or on a plain majority vote, or on absolute or modified unanimity, it can remove at least some of the grounds for argument. But the only real way of solving problems is for the whole team together to be determined to find the will of God for their situation, and to take the time to agonize, to discuss, to study the Bible, to seek the wisdom of others, and to pray together; and above all to be genuinely open to the possibility that God can still bring them to a common mind, if that is what they really desire.

Problems in renewing established teams

It must be said that teams can also come to an end in apparent failure for a number of perfectly good reasons. The break-up of a team does not necessarily mean that things have gone badly wrong, nor that the problems described in the previous sections were the cause. In one suburban parish a well-established team of seven pastoral assistants completely disintegrated within a single year, for seven separate reasons: serious illness, spouse's illness, marital problems, moving away, and pressures from increasing responsibility at home, in secular work and in other church commitments. This was felt as a real blow by everyone involved, but in fact many of the team may well be able to take up the work again when their particular pressure is removed.

This case highlights the need already mentioned for time to be given to monitoring the team's own spiritual life and growth, and for sharing personal problems and pressures in a caring and supportive atmosphere. It highlights the extra responsibility of the Minister as the leader of the team. It also points to two other general problems; it is sometimes quite difficult to bring new members into an established team, and equally difficult to help people retire from the team without loss of face when other pressures indicate that retirement is desirable.

1. Bringing new members into the team
It is obviously desirable to find the right balance between constant turnover of members and having no change at all. A lay team of any kind that has become too old or tired or out

of touch can be just as bad a bottleneck as a Minister to whom the same comments apply. In many churches a measure of change is likely to occur as people move and as church officers change, even allowing for the fact that in some places church-wardens still serve for twenty years or more. There may well be a greater need for continuity in the team in areas where the population itself is barely changing; and a greater need to ensure at least some turnover in places where there is high mobility in the population and congregation. It is probably best to build change into the system from the very beginning and so allow a decent escape for those who want to pull out, or who cannot really cope, and also to make room for new members.

In a growing church, of course, the team itself is likely to be growing in numbers and changing its area of responsibility. An eldership team consisting of the leaders of the five house groups in a congregation of 100 will have to change to cope with twenty house groups and a congregation of four hundred. But where numbers are only growing slowly, or not growing at all, there will still be people moving in, or growing spiritually, who could make a useful contribution to the team. Many churches decide when first setting up their team to leave at least one or two places vacant; it should then be open for the team itself or the Church Council to make proposals for additions to be made. Some types of team obviously include church officers automati-cally; this makes it doubly important to take great care in choosing their successors. It may also be difficult if (for example) Readers are automatically members of the team; a new young Reader, or one who moves in from elsewhere, may be excellent as a Reader but may well not fit into the team.

It may also seem difficult to bring in new members if the team has itself grown spiritually as a result of its responsibilities, in just the same way as when the team first began it was difficult to see how they could really share with the clergy. It is important to work on the principle of looking for those with suitable gifts, even if they are very undeveloped, and finding a way of developing them. In some places there may be many 'training' roles in house groups, in youth work, or in pastoral teams of some kind, where people can be given a measure of responsibility. Some churches make a point of inviting potential members of the eldership to sit in on their meetings over a period of months, to see whether it is right to join them. This makes it easier to avoid wrong appointments, but obviously creates a further difficulty if the Minister or the team feel that it would not be right to go ahead. One church set up its own training course for all potential leaders, with some of the existing team involved on a regular basis. By the end of the year they had found two new members for the eldership, three potential house group leaders, a recruit for Reader training and a replacement for a churchwarden who had died quite unexpectedly.

2. Retirement from the team

One writer has commented, 'Appeals to older elders to make way are often heeded by those who have the most valuable contribution still to make, and ignored by those who cannot see that their day is over'.[9] If everyone is happy and relationships are good, there is no problem. The older member, or the one who is under pressure of some kind, will either volunteer to pull out or will welcome the suggestion that he do so. But relationships are not always easy, and many churches have found it helpful, as soon as their scheme was formalized, to build into it some provision for retirement. Some have opted for automatic retirement after three or five years, with or without a year off before any possibility of reappointment. The year off need not be wasted. In fact, it can give the individual time to rethink priorities and to take on some extra reading or study, or a training course. And it is helpful to have a fixed reminder that no-one is indispensable.

Many have agreed on an age limit of seventy, perhaps partly bearing in mind the younger retirement age of the clergy. Depending on the workload of the team, this age limit can exclude people who still have a great deal to give, and it may be best to allow for exceptions to be made. In rural areas, or where the congregation is older than average, retired clergymen and other older people can be particularly useful members of the team.

10: Clarifying the vision

Change and growth always bring problems. In this case, the problems are mainly to do with fitting emerging gifts and developing relationships into traditional structures, or of adapting the traditional structures to cope with the new gifts and relationships.

Enthusiasts for change are almost always impatient, and they need to recognize that other people, and the institutions to which they belong, often have a natural resistance to change. But even where there is a willingness to accept change, there are bound to be growing pains. Part of the pain arises from institutional inertia, and the longer there has been no change, the more intense the pain can be. Part of the pain is due to the sheer cussedness of human nature, and excessive enthusiasm can sometimes actually generate an increased level of resistance to whatever change is being proposed!

Our thesis has been that change is necessary, even if pain is involved. If the church is to become and to be the gospel community which Christ calls it to be, some kind of renewed corporate local leadership is essential. For this to happen, four key principles must be recognized and adhered to: there must be a clear vision of where we want to go; our vision must be based on biblical principles; it must be socially and culturally appropriate; and people *must* be given time to come to terms with the changes involved, and accept them willingly.

The vision – corporate local leadership

The vision can be usefully clarified by looking first at the totally impossible job-description traditionally given to the solo Minister. A group of clergy were once asked to put together a vocational leaflet to be called *Wanted: Leaders in Tomorrow's*

Church. After a good summary of the personal qualities required, it sets out to describe the work:

> He will be a leader in the church's worship and a man of prayer, whose oversight encourages others to discover and exercise their vocation and gifts.
>
> He will be a planner and thinker, who communicates a vision of future goals and who seeks with others to achieve them.
>
> He will be a pastor and spiritual director, who is skilled in understanding, supporting and reconciling both groups and individuals.
>
> He will be a prophet, evangelist and teacher, who proclaims and witnesses to the gospel, and who makes available today the riches of the church's tradition and experience.
>
> He will be an administrator and co-ordinator, with responsibility for the Christian management and organization of the local church's resources

Clearly this is what most Ministers see as needing to be done if the church is to be the church. No doubt most church members still think that this is what their Minister should be doing. But few clergy have the gifts, and none have the time, to fulfil every section of that job-description except in a very small-scale and static operation. If the Minister tries to do everything on his own, the work will be limited to what one man on his own can do – a recipe for stagnation rather than for growth. One man on his own cannot enable, equip, pastor and teach the whole local church for the whole range of tasks to which it is called, unless either it is a very small church or he and it both have a very limited vision of what mission means. If 'every-member' ministry is to become a reality, leadership in the local church has to be corporate: pastors and teachers, overseers, elders in the plural – the title hardly matters. What really matters is that it should be a team, never one man on his own.

This impossible job immediately becomes much more possible as soon as the one man is transformed into a corporate leadership, as soon as you read 'they' instead of 'he':

> *They* will lead the church's worship . . . encourage others to develop their gifts

They will plan, and think . . .
They will be pastors . . .
They will bring the Word of God to the people . . .
They will co-ordinate the work of the body.

'They' – between them – not necessarily all doing everything, but between them bringing their varied gifts to bear upon the great variety of tasks required for leadership in the local church.

The vision – biblical pattern and principle

The church lives in the permanent tension between being a social institution nearly two thousand years old and being the pilgrim people of God: the tension between form and freedom. In order to see what particular form or forms will most helpfully allow the necessary freedom for the church's mission to develop appropriately in each place, it is necessary to summarize the patterns and principles of leadership as we see them in the teaching and example of Jesus, and the teaching and experience of his early followers.

1. The form of local leadership
The New Testament, as we have seen, knows of no such thing as one-man leadership in the local church. Everywhere the local leadership was in the hands of a team of local people. Whatever variations in the form of leadership existed, the key biblical principle is that it was corporate.

2. The function of local leadership
This is more important than the form it takes in any one place. The important thing is that the form must not prevent the team as a whole fulfilling its proper function of pastoral oversight of the congregation. This oversight includes all aspects of pastoral care and teaching, as well as the leadership and management of the local church's affairs.

The gift of teaching is specially required of church leaders in the Pastoral Epistles. They must uphold sound doctrine and refute error; they must also be trainers, equipping other Christians both for the work of ministry in general (Eph. 4:12) and also particularly for passing on the faith to the next generation of leaders and teachers (2 Tim. 2:2). This does not of course mean that all elders have to preach; teaching is not limited to sermons or lectures – it is also done in small groups and in one-to-one situations. With several 'teachers' in every local church, it becomes possible to help members at any intellectual level apply their minds to their faith to the maximum capacity. People can then be expected to understand their faith better than their favourite hobby, which is seldom the case today, and so contribute more effectively as Christians in their places of work or leisure.

Local church leaders are also pastors, and this too is clearly a shared responsibility. They are to guard and guide the flock (1 Tim. 3:5; 1 Pet. 5:2; Acts 20:28). They have particular responsibility to care for the weaker members of the fellowship, and to pray for the sick. Where some part of this pastoral burden is too great for them to carry, they need to 'turn this responsibility over to others, who are known to be full of the Spirit and wisdom' (Acts 6:3). This passage may not necessarily establish the need for a diaconate alongside an eldership, but it does give a positive precedent for the principle of delegation!

As teachers, the church leaders are responsible for maintaining sound doctrine, and as pastors, they are responsible for maintaining the moral behaviour of the church. Where necessary this responsibility must include discipline in both areas.

Finally, local church leaders are also managers. The title 'manager' may at first sight seem unspiritual, but the New Testament language used about local leadership certainly includes it. The gift of administration, the title of steward, both relate to this aspect of leadership. Leaders are required to 'rule the church well' (1 Tim. 5:17); they need to have demonstrated their capacity to rule or manage the church by their successful rule or management of their home and family life. A happy church, like a happy home, is one where a balance is struck which enables each member to contribute to the corporate life effectively. It is neither a dictatorship nor a democracy. It is not authoritarian, but there is nonetheless an authority which is accepted and freely recognized, and valued for the framework it provides. This element of authority in the church, as in a growing family, will need to be expressed in a variety of styles, according to the maturity, expectations and needs of the congregation. Jesus spoke about 'faithful and wise managers' (Lk. 12:42) who do their work efficiently. They will 'bring out of their storeroom new treasures as well as old' (Mt. 13:52).

Good management means thinking ahead, instead of constantly being forced to react to crises, so it has a bearing upon the way teaching and pastoring are carried out. The pastor who thinks in good management terms will be concerned to ensure that the system can deliver proper pastoral care and support, whatever needs emerge. It will require continual development of the pastoral gifts of others, rather than allowing all pastoral needs to be focused on himself. The teacher who thinks in good management terms will know what courses are available from the wider church, and will also know what sort of training is likely to be appropriate for each member to equip them most effectively for their ministry in the church or the world.

3. The character and attitude of local leadership
People learn more from what they see than from what they hear and if what they see contradicts what they hear, they may learn nothing. This is therefore the most vital aspect of the biblical pattern. Leaders must be themselves mature in the faith, not shaken by every new fashion; they must be examples to their flock (1 Pet. 5:3); and they must exhibit the virtues listed in the Pastoral Epistles (1 Tim. 3:1–13; Tit. 1:6–9). Paul regularly called upon his readers to follow his example. Viscount Montgomery of Alamein described leadership as requiring a character that inspires confidence, as well as the capacity to rally men and women to a common purpose. Both these are part of Christian leadership.

But the unique extra required of Christian leaders is a wholly Christ-like attitude to leadership: leaders are to be servants, like their master. Any sign of a domineering attitude is denounced by Jesus (Mk. 10:37–45) and rebuked by Peter (1 Pet. 5:1–5). Leaders have to follow the example of Jesus. He had all authority in heaven and earth, he demonstrated it in every sphere of life, and asserted it at times in ways that would have been blasphemous in a mere human. But he was 'among you as one who serves' (Lk. 22:27); he was 'gentle and humble of heart' (Mt. 11:29); he washed the feet of the disciples – the work of a menial slave – and commanded them to follow his example.

This attitude is in complete contrast to the world's normal pattern of leadership, but it is essential in the church not just because Jesus demands it, but also because it is part of the nature of the gospel. In the end Jesus sacrificed himself for his people; leaders in the church have to be willing to give themselves – not often literally, perhaps – but in various real and costly ways. The high-profile autocratic style, and the totally undemanding, non-directive approach are equally unsatisfactory. The way of Jesus means a constant tension between the attitude of humble service and the need to give the sort of lead which will motivate and enable the whole church to move ahead. It is always difficult to find the right balance. A team can become just as authoritarian as the traditional Minister on his own. But a team is more likely to ask itself the question, 'Is our attitude right?' and it is less likely to become isolated from the people and thereby insulated from their views.

The vision – socially and culturally appropriate

We have already indicated the need for variety in the way local leadership is developed. It must be appropriate to its local culture, and to the state of development of the local church.

1. *The cultural variety*

The Western church has at last woken up to the need for indigenous leadership in the churches of Africa, Asia and Latin America. We have seen some of the dangers of imposing on them, even unconsciously, our own Western cultural assumptions. But we have failed to translate this back into our own situation, and to realize that class and education, as well as tradition and culture, create an almost infinitely varied pattern. Some middle-class congregations are strongly tied to tradition, while others are eager for change. Some villages have been virtually taken over by incoming commuters; others retain an almost feudal expectation of their local squire; others have become havens for the retired. In each of these types, people will have different expectations of the village church, and will want to contribute to it in different ways.

Urban Priority Areas are not a homogeneous group either. They vary greatly in the extent to which they are 'a community of the left-behind' (David Sheppard's phrase), in the extent to which they contain 'pockets of gentrification' – from which the leadership in the local church often seems to be drawn – and in their own cultural and ethnic mix. The local church in UPAs varies even more then the rural church; sometimes it is a fair cross-section of the local community; sometimes it is not – and in extreme cases many of its leaders and members have already moved out of the area.

Any Minister who wants to develop a genuinely indigenous leadership team has to take account of this social and cultural variety. He needs to take account too of the significant differences between working-class and middle-class ways of reaching and making decisions, and of developing and maintaining relationships. If his own background, or his college training, makes his whole approach different from that of the congregation, he will have to learn new ways. The evidence presented to the Archbishop's Commission on UPAs suggests that it is 'the consistently middle-class presentation of the gospel and style of church life which creates the gulf between it and most working-class people'.[1] The Minister needs also to take account of the present expectations of the congregation, and at least to be aware of the expectations of the local community, because where these are substantial – where the church still has a significant civic or communal role – the opportunities this provides must not be neglected. In practice, all this means that the church has to be willing to look at itself critically; to analyse its own make-up and compare itself with the make-up of the local community. The Minister and other leaders also need to examine themselves critically: to check that the way they are working is appropriate to the local culture, to look at the style of their worship and preaching, and how they consult with others, reach decisions and then communicate them to the congregation.

2. Variety based on size of congregation

The church needs to learn from the secular world, that the appropriate management style is likely to vary according to the size of the organization. Eddie Gibbs in his book on church growth suggests that comparing the way local church leadership needs to work with the equivalent industrial operation of a similar size can offer some useful pointers as to where problems and pressures are most likely to arise.[2] Where the congregation is smaller than sixty-five, the leader has to operate like a foreman, able himself to do everything that needs to be done (and in the church often finding himself actually doing it!). Between sixty-six and 150 the parallel is with the supervisor, with many tasks delegated to others. But because the church is a voluntary organization, and people run away from the discipline of being tied to a particular task and held accountable if it is not done, the supervisor in the church is always under great pressure to check everything himself, and to oversee virtually every decision, down to the least detail. He may actually insist himself on retaining this degree of oversight, thus adding overwork and frustration to inefficiency.

At the next level upwards, with 151–450 members, the leader needs to adopt the style of middle management. There has to be real delegation and trust as well as proper reporting and accountability. At this level the need for assistant full-time staff becomes paramount either in the administrative field, or else to take over one or more major areas of responsibility – or more likely both, if the work is to go forward smoothly.

Finally, in churches with more than 450 members, the Minister is effectively in a senior management position, and each member of his full-time team, and probably some of those in part-time leadership, will have clearly defined areas of personal responsibility.

Secular management also has something to teach the church in the area of delegating decision-making and creating a sense of involvement, in ways appropriate to the size of the organization. The good manager knows that this depends mainly upon good decision-making procedures, including appropriate consultation and effective two-way communication from management to shop-floor and vice versa. The bigger the numbers, the more difficult it is to achieve, but it can be done. The giant IBM Corporation, whose turnover is now 200 times as big as thirty years ago, gives every employee a thorough training and a task which will stretch them without breaking them. Everyone's ideas for improvement of their service are welcomed. Every employee, from receptionist to chief executive, is seen as a key 'salesperson'. Each is committed to the same aim – not selling a piece of hardware, but forging a lasting personal relationship with the customer.

The church has a lot to learn from the best of secular management practice, but this is a long way from slavishly adopting any secular insights which seem convincing. They must first be brought alongside the biblical principles referred to already, and if necessary be judged by them. The whole structure of leadership must then be seen as under the Lordship of Christ. When Christ is truly the Head of the Church, no one individual and no one group can reign over the body, in the dominant way that is often seen as necessary in secular institutions. The church has to find appropriate models of leadership which enable and facilitate the increasing development of every member. In some places, the leadership may well need to be more dominant and visible than others, but everywhere it needs to be mainly indigenous and therefore able to relate effectively to the local culture.

The vision – time for change

There are many indications that the time for major changes in local church leadership has now come. In many denominations the number of professional full-time clergy has fallen, and in some it is still falling. But the work expected of them grows greater rather than less. In many denominations in the UK, and still more round the world, there is a movement towards corporate leadership. There has been an explosion in opportunities for lay training of various kinds in the last ten years in the UK on a quite unprecedented scale, so more people are now beginning to be more capable of the sort of work required.[3] There is a new theological openness to the idea of local eldership, and what seems to be a movement of the Holy Spirit, nudging the churches in this direction. It is indeed time for change.

But change needs to be given time; it is no good rushing it. Trying to force changes through too quickly can be counterproductive in at least three ways: it is very likely to antagonize those who are deeply set in a traditional way of thinking; it may put excessive pressures on those newly involved, before they are capable of bearing them; and it may even mean that the wrong approach to shared leadership is adopted, thus almost guaranteeing failure. Time spent in preparation is seldom, if ever, wasted. Time needs to be allowed for this new way of thinking to become accepted in the local community, in the congregations, and among the clergy and the institutional structures of the church, and then time must be allowed for training.

1. Changing the expectatons of the local community
Traditional attitudes to the church can often make it more difficult for the church to do its work. The community so often

identifies the church with the Vicar, the Minister or the Priest, simply because of his professional position. It expects him to play an active part in a long list of secular activities – and there may well be good work to be done, whether on flower festival committees or motorway protest action groups. There are always pastoral contacts, and often warring factions to be reconciled!

But this sort of demand can eat up the Minister's time, and distract him from building up church members. Worse still, it makes it more difficult for the community to recognize lay Christians as capable of having a pastoral or indeed any other specifically Christian role in the community.

Meanwhile, most ordinary people have an image of the Minister – both his person and his purpose – which is far removed from what we have been describing. When they turn to the church in a crisis or for one of the 'rites of passage', it is the Vicarage door on which they knock, and they expect to find behind it their traditional image of a Vicar, a compound made up in various proportions from the five-minute slot on radio and the caricature television clergyman. They may be completely baffled and even unnecessarily hurt if their expectations are not met in something like the traditional manner.

These expectations can be changed in two ways. First, by actually seeing new ways of working in practice. The initial shock and surprise wears off quite quickly when people become aware of the reality of shared leadership in the local church. The appointment of an efficient church secretary or administrator, even on a part-time basis, in a church office can have a dramatic effect in making it easier for questions to be answered and important needs met by someone other than the Vicar!

Secondly, there are plenty of opportunities for presenting a different image through the media. Christians working in local or national newspapers and radio and television, and those who supply them with news and other material, can have a big influence in either reinforcing the traditional image, or in gradually changing it. This is particularly important because effective lay leadership teams are still only just beginning to be known locally and the increasing volume of output in local newspapers and especially local radio provides many opportunities for new and successful ideas to be given a much wider airing. The massive response to the Lent 1986 programme, *What on earth is the Church For?* shows what the potential audience can be.

Local papers and local radio are generally hungry for news, provided it is properly presented to them. In general, it is churches with shared leadership which are growing, which are achieving something in their neighbourhood, and all this can be made into news, even good news! It may take time, but the general climate of opinion *can* be changed.

2. Changing the congregation's expectations

Progress clearly depends upon changing the way the congregation thinks. The traditional view of the one-man ministry may be so deeply rooted that change seems impossible. Many may be hurt, and feel threatened, by any talk of change. An extended period of teaching on church, gifts and ministry is likely to be required, and this can be done through sermons, house groups and church meetings. A year may be needed – perhaps two or three – if this is unfamiliar territory. It is essential that everyone gets used to the idea that the church is 'us' rather than 'them', that 'all of us are involved in ministry', that every member has a God-given gift to be used in his service, and that the full development of the life and work of the church requires some form of corporate leadership.

In some places even two or three years may not be enough to prepare the ground for eldership in a full sense. But even where many in the church are eager to push ahead as fast as possible, it is almost certainly right to hasten slowly, to build secure foundations and to be sure that everyone is thinking along the same lines. Several Ministers underlined this: 'We have always moved slowly; we have taught, explained, persuaded. There are always some people whose security is threatened by change. We were determined to carry the whole congregation with us'.

During this exploratory educational period, it will almost certainly be helpful to arrange one or more special occasions – for the Church Council or the whole congregation – when a team from another reasonably similar church can explain their own experience and answer questions. In some churches the main input on the subject, the main vision for development, may come from the Minister; in others, there may be considerable lay enthusiasm. In either case, it will be helpful if the Minister can discuss the issue regularly with churchwardens, deacons, Readers, and the Church Council in an open-ended way, so that all can contribute to the development of a proper plan, and also to ensure that there is the maximum opportunity for congregational reaction to be heard. The church may not be ready to move very far, and it may well be wrong to press it to do so.

There should be no sense of shame or failure in saying, 'We are not ready for an eldership. Let us therefore strengthen our standing committee and really make it give time to policy. Or let us set up a pastoral team. Or let us develop lay involvement in this area and in that. Or let us form a pastoral committee within the PCC, or the diaconate, to meet regularly with the Minister to share in pastoral concerns. Or let us develop our heads of departments, or let us have a 'staff-meeting' with churchwardens and Readers and if necessary free them from some of their other commitments so that they can give time to being together.' All these things can be done within the existing structures, so there is no absolute need for official approval to be given for any of them. But for the avoidance of any doubt or suspicion, it is obviously desirable that church officers and congregation always know what is going on, and are kept in regular touch.

There are of course some places where church officers and Church Councils see their main task as the upkeep of the building and the continuing provision of its services. Wherever possible, it is best to work within the accepted structures, and help existing office-holders enlarge their understanding of their own role and of the mission of the church. This may prove impossible. Sometimes it may even be undesirable. Beautiful ancient monuments can only be maintained if there are people willing to give a great deal of time, skills and enthusiasm to the task, and it may be quite wrong to expect those with that sort of gift also to be involved in the pastoral work of the church. Their specific ministry needs to be affirmed, and it may be right to set up a parallel system for shared pastoral and spiritual responsibility. This should only be done with their full understanding and approval. On rare occasions, if the church officers are totally opposed to any such development, it may be necessary to wait patiently and continue teaching about 'every-member' ministry and shared leadership, until either they change their mind or others are elected to their office who take a more favourable view.

It is of course possible to start the ball rolling without the full understanding and consent either of church officers or of congregation. It may sometimes be right to move very gently into some of the early stages without raising too many questions. It may for instance be appropriate to develop an informal pastoral team, or to arrange more regular meetings with church officers and to begin to feed pastoral and policy matters into their agenda, without raising anyone's doubts by talking too theoretically about shared leadership. In the early stages it may in any case not be at all clear which way forward is appropriate. But even for these informal moves, a measure of growing congregational understanding is likely to be helpful. This becomes absolutely essential as soon as there is any question of formalizing arrangements on any of the lines indicated earlier, and the sooner such education begins, the more likely it is that people will find the new ideas acceptable, and therefore be able to participate positively in the whole process.

3. Changing the expectations of the clergy
We have already described why many clergy are at first hostile to any talk of shared leadership; it challenges their legal position, it is a threat to their status, and it raises many practical problems. There is a fourth and vital factor: most of them have grown up within a particular pattern of role-expectation, and they are apparently being asked to abandon suddenly something which has been central to their whole life and understanding of their vocation. They can be helped to change their minds in much the same way as their congregations – by seeing examples, by persuasion, and by propaganda!

First, the example of churches where shared leadership is developing needs to be publicized. There is already a trickle of articles in the church press and theological journals. Individual stories of shared leadership have been referred to in a growing number of books over the last ten to fifteen years. It is never easy for anyone to say, 'Come and see what we're doing – we think we've got something worthwhile to share with you'. Such talk sounds arrogant, and in practice can very easily lead to the sort of pride that goes before a fall. Nevertheless, the presence of a growing number of churches which are moving towards shared leadership, and their willingness to share their experience honestly and openly with others, either in writing or personally, is a key part of the process.

Next, persuasion. Again, books and articles have been appearing in increasing quantity which argue the case on practical and biblical grounds. There is now in fact a remarkable mismatch between theory and practice. Many clergy, and indeed many theological college tutors, bishops and other church leaders give the impression that they are more or less convinced of the theoretical arguments for some form of shared local leadership. But it takes time for reality to catch up with theological conviction, in this as in many other areas of Christian experience. The persuasion process therefore has to continue, with greater refinement, particularly with a more thorough analysis of what is actually happening at the grass roots. The research on which this book is based took a very broad-brush approach. We hope that others will carry it further, and in greater depth. It would for example be useful to examine the effects on the development of eldership teams of different types of congregation – social background, churchmanship and denomination – and of different types of Minister.[4]

Thirdly, there needs to be propaganda. The idea must be propagated if it is to be heard more widely, and for this there is no advocate so useful as a former opponent. One Vicar in Ely Diocese for some time resisted any consideration of the diocesan scheme for elders. He was then persuaded to try it out, and within a year of his first elders being commissioned he wrote to the patrons of his church, saying that when they were looking for his successor it was imperative that they find a man committed to the principle of shared leadership and willing to work with the lay team in his parish. Those who are committed to the idea must be prepared to speak out boldly. But to be heard they must speak both with deep biblical conviction and from practical experience.

Much can be done through informal Ministers' fraternals, through casual contacts at conferences and celebrations, and through the provision already made for in-service training. More study materials and more courses could almost certainly be made available if interested people asked for them.

Taking a longer-term view, the principle of shared leadership must somehow be squeezed into the crowded curriculum which those preparing for ordained ministry already have to digest. Perhaps more importantly, just as some people are having to learn to purge their conversation of unconscious anti-feminism, so all those involved with training need to purge their lecture and seminar notes of material which still assumes the one-man ministry as the norm.

The vision – a two-fold local ministry?

The development of local leadership teams, and some of the pressures and problems they have experienced have now been surveyed. There is considerable evidence that in many cases both the problems and the pressures could have been avoided if a clear distinction between 'elders' and 'deacons' had been made. In some cases teams were trying to fulfil both roles and not surprisingly found it was too much for them; in others people described as elders were in fact doing diaconal work or were in fact only equipped for diaconal work. The right way forward might well be for churches to think in terms of having a long-term plan to develop a team of local deacons as well as a team of local elders, both working alongside the professional full-time ministry. This could be just as helpful where a congregation has one or several full-time staff as where one full-time Minister serves a number of separate congregations.

In many churches the new pastoral eldership teams are very frequently trying to do too much, or finding that they are expected to do too much. This pressure may not be felt quite so seriously in a small church. A small team can fairly easily share in the whole range of what had previously been a full-time Minister's work. But in medium-sized or larger churches or those where mission is taken seriously and growth is beginning, a single all-purpose local team can be just as limiting to growth as a solo minister, and because they lack his professional training they may feel the pressure of being unable to cope even more deeply. Some teams have indeed broken down as a result, and others after an enthusiastic start have drifted back into a maintenance-only position where they contribute little or nothing to the forward movement of the church and simply become an extra talking-shop.

This confusion occurs in a somewhat different way in churches which have always had deacons – whether they have seen themselves as under the Minister or as in some way 'over' him because they had appointed him! When some of their number have become elders and begin to share in the pastoral and spiritual leadership and oversight of the church there seems little left for the remaining deacons to do. The elders are often overloaded and the deacons frustrated. Some Baptist churches avoid this by deliberately leaving the deacons a pastoral task and either transferring their administrative and financial responsibilities to the secretary and treasurer as individuals, or retaining these tasks within the diaconate but entrusting them to two or three particular individuals who may well not share in the pastoral work of the other deacons.

1. Separate functions and different gifts

Both in the early church and in the ministry of Jesus himself, it is clear that the pressure of the pastoral needs of the crowds was constantly threatening to swamp the ministry of the word. This is a clear pointer to the need for a separation of functions. But it seems equally obvious that the gifts necessary for leadership in the local church (local elders) are by no means necessarily the same as the gifts necessary for diaconal service in the name of the church, whatever form that service takes, because the actual work involved is different. This difference has been fully recognized by the Roman Catholic Church in America, where the training for permanent deacons is seen not only as including basic doctrine and the ability to think theologically about issues, but as requiring a much stronger emphasis on the particular type of work to which the deacon is called. The seminary-based model simply creates religious professionals. Deacons must be equipped to serve in the name of Christ with caring love in their chosen sphere of service. They are in no way alternative leaders in the church. They may have a public, liturgical role as assistants in reading, prayer and administering the sacraments, but they are not involved in teaching or oversight.

The relevance of this proposed separation of function is well illustrated by the experience of 'local eldership' in the Diocese of Ely, where thirteen such teams have been developed with official support in the last ten years, consisting of seventy local elders (compared with eighty-three Readers in seventy-two parishes). In practice very few of them are doing any of the work associated with presbyters in the New Testament. None are authorized to preach (unless also a Reader) and the only ones who share in the oversight or leadership of the congregation are those who are also churchwardens. Their role is almost entirely 'pastoral' (within the congregation) or 'charitable' (within the local community), or a mixture of the two, usually with some liturgical involvement as well. A recent review recommended among other things: (i) that authorized lay ministry along the lines of the present eldership should be

encouraged throughout the diocese and that they should be
called Lay Pastoral Assistants; (ii) that a 'ministry team' should
be set up in each parish or group of parishes to include NSMs
and Readers as well as Lay Pastoral Assistants. In several other
dioceses Pastoral Assistants have been or are being recognized.
Their selection and training are different from those provided
for Readers and for NSMs because the work to which they are
being called is different.

It is worth observing that the pattern suggested above is quite
similar to that which emerged during the second century, in
places where local presbyters shared with the local bishop in
the responsibilities of teaching, leadership and oversight, while
a team of deacons worked under him in the whole field of
pastoral need. In today's terms that would include not only the
pastoral care of the church's own members, but also co-operation with other voluntary organizations and local social
services.

2. Recognizing a local diaconate

There is a widespread concern about any unnecessary proliferation of titles, which would apply particularly to a local diaconate. If their role is service, why do they need a title at all?
Will they not inhibit the rest of the laity? Will they not devalue
the service of the 'ordinary Christian'? Such questions could
equally well be asked of the early church, and we can see
pointers to what their answer would have been in Acts chapter
6 and in the Pastoral Epistles. Today's answer would have been
on similar lines, that of course all Christians can do this sort of
work without a title, but there are substantial arguments in
favour of having a recognized team at the centre of it all.

At the most practical level, unless there is some sort of
organized team some things may not be done because everyone
assumes that someone else will be doing it. Even where there
is a good caring congregation a great many needs will still not
be met or will be overlooked completely for lack of organization. It is of course possible that once there is a pastoral team
the rest of the congregation will leave it all to them – just as
many at present leave it all to the Vicar 'because it's his job,
isn't it?' But one of the specific roles of a diaconal team is to
draw others into their work. Belonging to a formal team can
also help those actually involved in the work. Apart from the
training they have been given, whatever that may be, there

should be continuing benefit from regular team meetings in terms of mutual support and in-service training, and also the extra confidence which comes from having been commissioned by the church for the work.

There is also a benefit to those on the receiving end of their ministry. Many still feel that 'the church' has not taken an interest unless the Vicar has called. Others may reasonably ask, 'Who is this Mrs Smith sticking her nose into my problems?'

These complaints are less likely if there is a team of people called by the local church to this kind of service. If everyone knows that these people have been chosen as suitable, that they have been trained and are accountable in some way, they have at least some guarantee of their competence, discretion and reliability. There need be nothing exclusive about the ministry of such a team of deacons. In terms of the evidence presented in Chapter 8 the picture would be one where a church had developed both a pastoral team of deacons and an eldership of presbyters.

3. The scope of a local diaconate

There is no reason for a local diaconate to be limited either to the local pastoral work which preceding paragraphs might seem to imply or to the responsibility for finance and administration which is normal in some denominations today. Local diaconal service could be expected to extend outwards into a whole variety of more specialized areas of social and community need. This could be in association with other churches or in partnership with state agencies or other voluntary organizations which seem increasingly unable to cope adequately with the sheer volume of need, and are often glad to welcome involvement from the church provided such involvement is reliable, regular and in some way accountable.

If we envisage a local diaconate developing on these lines it would be very natural for some of its members to move on or to be called on by the church into part-time or even full-time paid work in their particular field of service. An increasing number of local churches of all denominations now have part-time or full-time paid lay pastoral workers of various kinds, and this is entirely a matter for the local church. But people of this kind would also form a very natural recruiting ground for those whom the wider church might wish to call into a full-time stipendiary diaconal ministry.

11: Conclusion

In an attempt to unite the visionary with the practical this book has narrowed its focus from a general description of Christianity as the gospel community, a unique kind of religious association, down to a discussion of one particular development in that association in a number of local churches in contemporary Britain. The argument has been made as sharp as possible in order to emphasize the potential significance of the development of a corporate style of leadership for recovering a clearer expression of the church as the gospel community. But the case which has been presented could easily be misinterpreted. Our conclusion therefore must ensure that the reader does not come to some *wrong* conclusions!

The importance of leadership

We have described the church as neither a hierarchy nor a democracy, but as a community led by the Spirit in which the charismatic reality is a multiplicity of gifts bestowed upon the whole Body. Unless each part is working properly (Eph. 4:16) the true guidance and leadership of the Holy Spirit is not fully effective in producing growth to maturity. Yet in the same passage Paul indicates the existence of particular leadership gifts which, if fully recognized and used, will enable the whole Body to undertake its proper ministry. Clericalism has become a major obstacle to renewal because of a false belief that leadership gifts are restricted to the ordained ministry and are in fact bestowed by the act of ordination itself. The result is that in many local churches the single ordained minister is looked to as the sole focus of leadership. But nowhere in the New Testament are leadership gifts confined to those who hold the office of bishop, presbyter or deacon. Although such gifts may be recognized by the church, and confirmed and strengthened in the individual, by means of the laying on of hands with prayer, there is no biblical basis for meeting the church's needs for authority, holiness, competence and leadership in its ministry (see pp. 20–23 above) from the clergy alone. The choice is not between a professional ordained leadership and a leaderless chaos: there are good grounds for concluding from the evidence presented in this book that many local churches are capable of producing their own corporate leadership within which the ordained ministry has a crucial and creative part to play.

The place of the laity

It has been necessary to use the traditional terminology of clergy and laity to make this book intelligible without requiring the reader to make constant efforts of mental readjustment. But the truth is that this language is itself the product of clericalist assumptions. All the laity are 'clergy' in the original meaning of the word, and the clergy in the restricted modern sense are certainly all included within the laity. The term 'lay' in the church ought never to imply 'amateur' or 'non-professional'; to give any of the ministries within the church the prefix 'lay' is meaningless. There should be no lay pastors or lay elders or lay preachers, only pastors and elders and preachers. The last bastion of those who rally to the defence of clericalism in these days is the proposition that the true ministry of the laity is in the world from which their essential witness will be withdrawn if they are to become pre-occupied with running the church. But of course no-one, least of all the clergy, should be left to 'run the church', and everyone, clergy included, should be witnessing in the world! There will always be some people, both at national and at local level, who will have to devote a great deal of their time to the practical and domestic affairs of the church as a human organization. But everyone must be concerned with its life as a community. The gospel, based on a biblical understanding of mission, can only be proclaimed by a community. Isolated, individual Christian witness means little, particularly in a pluralistic society, unless it is an integral part of a fellowship where the gifts of the Spirit are producing growth in faith and love. The ministry of pastoring, teaching and encouragement which is used to this end is not a diversion from mission, because mission is not defined by what happens when Christians are dispersed, any more than worship is defined by what happens when they gather together. The coming together is not to form a club, or a society for the maintenance of cultic acts, or a historic buildings conservation group, but to be the gospel community, expecting the kingdom and exercising the gifts of the Spirit.

The priority of worship

The kingdom of God comes through prayer, through the moving of the Spirit, through God breaking into human affairs in judgment and in deliverance, bringing salvation to those who 'sit in darkness and in the shadow of death' (Lk. 1:79). For this reason worship is not only fundamental to Christian mission, it is the distinguishing characteristic of it. To reach a needy world all the resources of human imagination and compassion and endeavour must be employed. But the gospel community witnesses to the activity of God. Worship therefore does not mean retreating into the sanctuary in an attitude of prayerful, passive helplessness. It means becoming the Body through which Christ can come to the world today. Certainly the needs of the world include specifically religious needs. Even, or perhaps especially, in a materialistic society men and women are seeking a sense of the transcendent power and majesty of God, an awareness of the beauty of holiness in worship, and a response to the magnetic call of the eternal realm. Such religious needs are often met in acts of worship where music and colour and drama and ritual are employed with great effect. But to think of this as the essence of Christian worship, or the centre of our sacrifice of praise, is to turn Christianity into cultic religion and worship into symbolic gestures. The beauty of holiness shines through the starving refugee and the transcendent power of God works through the hand which offers a bowl of food. This is the re-interpretation of cultic religious language which Jesus gave to the religious people of his own day.

The significance of structures

Finally, it would be wrong to conclude from this book that corporate leadership has been proposed as one more recipe for structural reform. Doubtless it is already being seized upon by some who are ever looking for fresh ways of saving the church by reorganization. We have come across churches where an extension of ministerial authority to a team or group has been incorporated harmoniously into existing structures; others where it has been set up alongside them as an additional and potentially conflicting element; others again where corporate leadership is part and parcel of a new alternative structure which has been created over against the traditional form of the local church. The work of the Spirit must not be confused with structural reform. Wherever the new life of the Spirit flows into the church it is inevitable that some structural changes will occur. But whether this means renewal of what already existed, or its replacement, depends upon local circumstances. It is easy to suppose that the right thing is to adapt the existing structures, thus preserving as much continuity as possible. This is to over-look the profound gospel truth that the Spirit works by a process of death and resurrection. In some places the old order may actually have to disappear before the life of the gospel community can flourish. On the other hand it is equally easy to conclude that a complete break is always necessary, and to misapply the reference of Jesus to new wine needing fresh wineskins (Mt. 9:14–17). That is to attach too much significance to the structures, which are quite incidental to the gospel community. To return to the analogy of scaffolding round a building, we must not imagine that any structures for the church can be more than a temporary device, albeit a necessary and useful one in many cases. So long as the church continues to exist in the 'last days' the new creation of God's Spirit is working within the old order. The result is great diversity of response; the case studies included in the appendix demonstrate well that such diversity is beginning in some places to make Christians very aware of the provisional nature of the church's organization. There are now an increasing number of local churches who do not expect to be organized in the same way in five years' time because the members have woken up to the exciting fact that God is always leading them on to new things, that where there is life there is bound to be growth and change, and that it is fundamental to their calling as a gospel community to be ready for the coming of God's kingdom in unexpected ways.

Corporate leadership is therefore an important principle for the church's life and ministry, not just because it is an effective form of human organization but because it is more appropriate for a community which is led by the Spirit and is expecting the kingdom of God. Such leadership is God's gift to the church, and such a community is God's gift to the world in Jesus, the Founder and Finisher of our faith.

Appendix

Some examples of churches with corporate leadership

The descriptions which follow are all attempts to summarize briefly some of the circumstances in particular local churches which have led to some kind of experiment in shared leadership, and how this has subsequently developed. It is hoped that within the limits of space available each situation has been described fairly and accurately. The decision has been taken to keep them anonymous, although anyone with local knowledge might well be able to recognize one or other of them. For further examples drawn from various denominations and described in greater detail see:

A Kane, *Let There Be Life* (Marshalls, 1983)
M Saward, *All Change* (Hodder & Stoughton, 1983)
Ten Growing Churches ed.E Gibbs (Marc-Europe, 1984)
Ten New Churches ed.R Forster (Marc-Europe, 1986)

1. A team which 'failed'; but where lay leadership is growing well

A big northern parish with two churches, three clergy and a population of twenty thousand had a 'pastoral leadership team' in the seventies consisting of the clergy, churchwardens, two Readers, and four others holding specific posts in the church. It was quite useful as a consultative group, but when Arthur arrived in 1980, with a strong commitment to the biblical principle of corporate leadership, he quickly saw that the existing team were much too busy, and in some cases lacked the spiritual maturity, to exercise the sort of leadership role which the congregation needed.

The church grew in numbers, a third worship centre was opened up in a rented school building on the edge of a large council estate, and a fourth (part-time) member joined the staff. It soon became clear that the lay team could not keep up with the pace of events (and the daily staff-meeting) and it was agreed to disband it. At the same time there was a steady increase in various forms of lay responsibility on the pastoral side. From ten house groups in 1980 there were fifteen in 1983 and twenty-two in 1985: group leaders met once a quarter for a half-day of training, which allowed time for consultation on some of the wider issues in the church. Lay people have gradually taken on responsibility for training in evangelism and for the oversight of regular pastoral visiting, much of which is organized through the house groups. Planning and oversight of house group study material is now partly delegated to lay people, and others are beginning to share with the clergy in marriage preparation and in leading the regular Christian basics groups.

There are now a number a men who would be capable of sharing effectively in a central leadership team, but the most able are also those who are too busy in their secular jobs to give the time required, while others still lack sufficient spiritual maturity to cope in a congregation which includes a substantial charismatic presence. They are therefore concentrating on developing lay leadership further in all the individual departments of the church's life and work, recognizing that this may be the only way forward at present.

2. Lay elders alongside pastoral teams

Brian had developed a small informal pastoral team in his first inner-city parish; when he moved in 1982 to a more mixed neighbourhood he found a congregation with considerable leadership potential. His predecessor had laid good foundations for developing some form of eldership; several people were already helping to lead the worship: others were doing a part-time counselling course set up by St John's College, Nottingham. They agreed to spend time exploring the best way forward, with study groups and sermons on church and ministry, and they found tapes by Graham Cray of St Michael-le-Belfry in York particularly helpful. A small working group then put proposals to the PCC, which were discussed at a church day conference and implemented in 1984. These called for five 'neighbourhood pastoral teams', each with five or six members, covering the five distinct areas of the parish (and by agreement overlapping in part with adjoining parishes, where boundaries are illogical). Their main activity is a weekly house group in each area; they hope to subdivide the groups as numbers grow; the groups will gradually take on more of the visiting in their area.

The church as a whole is pastored by the eldership, consisting of the two clergy, one of the three Readers, and three others. The churchwardens are kept in close touch, but did not feel equipped to be involved in pastoral responsibility. The team meets for one evening each week for prayer, mutual support and personal sharing, and to discuss plans and policies. Once a month all the neighbourhood teams join them. Some of the other groups involved in ministry in different ways have felt slightly left out, and this is now under careful review.

The congregation had put forward a long list of possible names for both teams, and after extended consultation the clergy prepared two shorter lists, which the PCC approved. The neighbourhood teams are kept under regular review, with additions being made by the eldership when suitable people emerge or where gaps need to be filled. The eldership was initially commissioned for three years by the Vicar and Church Council, with the approval of the diocesan authorities. One member may be leaving shortly to pursue study on a local course, and another is considering ordination, so they are looking for one or two others (probably from the neighbourhood teams) to join them. They are keen to preserve the core of the present team, so that its growth may continue; they feel that the eldership is still in its very early stages of growing together, although it is already an effective sounding board for ideas, and helping usefully in dealing with problems and for working towards a right sense of priorities in the life of the church. It is contributing to an increase in pastoral care, but they also note real growth in all those involved in leadership at both levels. The congregation has grown by about twenty per cent since 1983.

3. A formal eldership structure

After two years' experience with an informal lay team, Chris started discussions in his flourishing suburban evangelical congregation which led to an agreed 'Charter for Eldership'. This was set up in 1977, and was designed to preserve the position of those with statutory responsibility while maximizing lay involvement in ministry. Thus the Vicar was declared to be 'presiding elder', with the right to veto any name proposed for inclusion in the eldership; Vicar and PCC had the right to disband the elderhsip and its continued existence would be subject to the approval of a new incumbent. The eldership was not to usurp the authority of the PCC in any way, but could make recommendations to it where appropriate. No-one except the clergy would be an elder simply because of holding office in the church – Readers might not have the right pastoral gifts, churchwardens might be too busy, and it was felt that a continuity was necessary, which would be upset by changes in those holding elected offices.

The main emphasis was on the team's collective role, in sharing pastoral care and oversight, and in maintaining unity and vision in the whole body through good communications at every level. This latter point grew in importance when a separate worship centre was set up in another part of the parish in 1979, and in the next year they were asked to take on the next door parish which had fallen on hard times. Some members of the eldership team also had an area of individual responsibility or specific oversight. It was agreed that the Vicar would appoint the elders after consultation with the PCC; their proposals turned out to be identical, even to the point that both lists left out the same name from the previous informal team. The Charter provided for an annual review, but in the first six years the only change was the addition of one member when the next parish joined them.

A major review took place in 1984, after Chris had spent a sabbatical term studying the experience of eldership in other parishes. He had concluded that the New Testament provided principles, but no standard patterns, and that the shape of any structures of ministry must be governed by the demands of the gospel and the current needs of each local church in its own cultural setting. Against this background, and with general satisfaction with their own experience, only marginal changes in the Charter were made. It was agreed that two members would retire each year, and take at least a year off before reappointment, to ensure a way in for new people; the new names are chosen by Vicar and PCC in consultation with the other elders. In alternate years, the whole Electoral Roll will be invited to make nominations, which will then be considered by the PCC. Their role has now been defined as 'exercising pastoral oversight in such a way as to draw out and develop the gifts and ministries of the church as a whole'. This includes supporting and caring for the clergy and other leaders, particularly the Area Fellowship leaders and Parish Visitors; acting as a focal point for unity in an active and expanding congregation; and working with clergy and others towards a shared vision and strategy for the church.

Over the years this group has found it essential to meet at least fortnightly, and their most convenient time is Saturday mornings at 8 am. Every third such meeting includes the Area Fellowship leaders.

4. The gradual approach

In 1980 David took on a town centre parish where everything spiritual had previously been kept rigidly in the Vicar's hands. He was convinced that a gradual process was most likely to produce good results. He therefore worked to create an atmosphere in which a variety of gifts were expected and indeed encouraged to emerge, and to deploy those gifts under careful supervision and with appropriate training, taking care to ensure that at all stages the PCC approved.

Some people began to lead the intercessions at parish communion; some to take communion to the housebound. Some later began to help plan special services, and later still to share in leading the services, or in speaking on special occasions. For all this there was training – one-to-one, or in small groups; recognition of gifts gradually emerging; encouragement; and of course the occasional mistake. A larger group was trained to lead a first-ever autumn series of house group meetings, which has been repeated in subsequent years with greater numbers, and in greater depth, so drawing more people into leadership. Others were slowly drawn in to helping with preparation for baptism, marriage and confirmation. By 1985, it was possible to have three separate adult Christian Basics

courses (preparation for confirmation) led entirely by lay
people, and for all the baptism preparation to be done by lay
teams of three people, who visit each family three times before
the event. A number of people have also been drawn into a
healing and counselling ministry which is linked with other
churches in the town.

Recently the whole congregation has been divided into six
geographical areas, with a 'Home Church' in each, which
replaces previous house groups and bible-study groups. Most
of them are led jointly by two couples, chosen by the clergy
and approved by the Church Council, who have 'emerged' as
suitable through the training and experience of the last four
years. Each Home Church, with a core of twelve to fifteen
regular members, has responsibility for pastoral visiting,
baptism preparation and general neighbourhood care in its
area.

In four years, a great number of gifts – including many in
areas not mentioned above – have been discovered, tested,
developed, trained, encouraged and used. They recognize that
most people's gifts are still at an early stage of growth; there
are not enough mature teachers, or pastoral skills, or gifts in
leading worship, but there are many people with emerging gifts
in all these areas. They expect that some of those now
exercising leadership gifts on a small scale in the Home Churches will develop a capacity in due course to share fully with
the clergy in the leadership of the whole congregation.

5. Lay pastors in a rural group

When Eddie became the vicar of four villages in the West
Country in 1981 he set about developing a team of lay pastors
based on his previous experience in East Anglia. One particular
concern was to hold together the pastoral and liturgical side of
the team's work, partly because in the rural context it is
expected that those who minister pastorally will also play a
leading part in the church's worship.

Eddie therefore laid his ideas before the four PCC's. These
included the need for the lay pastors to share in the whole
range of pastoral work while encouraging the development of
individual gifts; for the local congregations to have a major
role in selecting the team ('volunteers' and 'Vicar's nominees'
would be equally wrong); and for the team to be seen as

enabling the ministry of the whole congregation rather than being a substitute for it. Three of the PCC's gave general approval, and the fourth joined in later on. They were asked to suggest names of people whom they considered suitable, and the same names were put forward with remarkable unanimity. The Vicar then talked it through personally with each nominee, and one withdrew because of heavy business, family and other church commitments. There was then a three month training period led by the Vicar, including an introduction to leading worship and to basic pastoralia, followed by commissioning by the Bishop with maximum publicity to ensure that the local community knew who the pastors were and what they were being expected to do.

The team has met regularly to arrange services, to think ahead on evangelism and teaching in the church, and to deepen its pastoral understanding. Members began at once to share in pastoral visiting (including hospitals), in baptism and marriage interviews, in bereavement visits and other counselling. In all these areas experience has led to increasing capacity and their ministry has been increasingly valued not only in the parishes but by the Vicar. When the initial three year commission ended in 1985 the PCC's were unanimous in asking that all five should continue (four women and a man), and added another to the team. Before that one PCC had expressed its concern to the Bishop that they had no Eucharist when the Vicar went on holiday because a stand-in could not be found. They argued that in his absence the team corporately should have been able to take the Communion service as this was the central act of worship of the local church and they were already seen as sharing together in every aspect of the Vicar's work. The next time he was away they had the Bishop's permission to take the whole service excepting part of the Eucharistic Prayer, and to administer Communion from the reserved sacrament. Comments from the congregation were uniformly favourable.

In other areas their work has grown in depth; they have encouraged others to minister in a variety of ways both in church and in the community; they have grown in confidence both in leading worship and in explaining their faith. In this particular rural group a foundation has been laid for growth through more effective pastoral concern and involvement by leaders from within the local communities.

6. A parish church with three daughter churches

By 1980 the problems of this parish were those of growth. A population of fifteen thousand in an area including a village, a council estate, farmland, new private housing and older semi-detached and terraced housing, and a congregation approaching eight hundred produced formidable demands on the staff of three clergy. New members needed teaching; thirty or more house group leaders needed support and continuing training; an increasing number of people needed counselling over personal problems.

The first step was to form a team of Pastoral Leaders around Frank, the Vicar, at the parish church. They were selected by him in close consultation with churchwardens, staff and PCC, and commissioned early in 1981. For the first three years there was some uncertainty about their role, beyond each having a link with five or six house groups. A clearer structure has recently emerged in which three of the team have taken on areas of particular responsibility: one in overall charge of work with children and young people; one overseeing all aspects of evangelistic and missionary concern, including training in evangelism; one with special concern for the family life of the church. The other two have no specific area of work. One of the clergy at present acts as overseer of the house groups and nurture groups.

Development of lay leadership in the daughter churches has been on different lines, partly because they are smaller, and partly because it became clear that the most strategic use of the two assistant clergy was in areas of ministry in the parish as a whole. So each daughter church is largely run by Pastoral Leaders; the smallest has three, the others have one and two respectively, this being the number provided by God in each place with suitable gifts. Each group meets on its own and also separately with the Vicar. Preaching is planned centrally, and there are central administrative resources, but otherwise responsibility is local.

After five years, Frank commented on what they have learned: 'The demand on the time of the Pastoral Leaders is considerable. Clear definition of roles is vital to avoid waste of energy and overburdening. The length of time a Pastoral Leader is in office should be a matter of the spirit, not of law . . . I learned early on that the group had to be my number one priority . . . Some Pastoral Leaders may have a time "without portfolio" . . . This gives them "time to breathe" and wait on the Lord. They are still part of the team and often make the wisest contributions . . . The Vicar is learning to "let go", and however willing he still has blind spots . . . Laymen are learning to take on the responsibility for the direction of the church . . . Members of the congregation are exchanging what for them is an established view of leadership for an experimental one.'

Notes

Notes to chapter one: Can the churches be revived?

1 See O Chadwick, *The Victorian Church*, Black, 2nd edn 1972, vol ii pp 219–32.
2 Dr G Gaskell, quoted in *The Times*, 31 March 1986.
3 F van der Meer & C Mohrmann, *Atlas of the Early Christian World*, Nelson, 1966, map 2.
4 *The Documents of Vatican II*, ed W M Abbott, Chapman, 1966, p 4.
5 Under the Worship & Doctrine Measure 1975.
6 *All Are Called: Towards a Theology of the Laity*, CIO Publishing, 1985, p 3f.
7 *Faith in the City: A Call for Action by Church and Nation*, Church House Publishing, 1985, p 73.
8 D Jenkins, *The Protestant Ministry*, Faber, 1958, p 45.
9 J von Rohr, *Profile of Protestantism*, Dickenson Publishing, Belmont, Cal., 1969, p 208.
10 See e.g. the doubts expressed in *Faith in the City*, p 80.
11 D Clark, *The Liberation of the Church*, The National Centre for Christian Communities and Networks, Birmingham, 1984, p 83.
12 Ibid, p 86.
13 Quoted in Clark, op cit, p. 85.
14 Op cit, p 93.
15 G H Lang, *The Local Assembly: Some Essential Differences between Open and Exclusive Brethren considered Scripturally and Historically*, Raven Publishing, Belfast, 5th edn 1955.
16 W E Davies, *Rocking the Boat: The Challenge of the House Church*, Marshall Pickering, 1986.
17 E Vincent, *Something's Happening*, Marshall Pickering, 1984, p 47. Restoration is sometimes spoken of as something closely akin to revival or renewal, but it definitely includes the introduction of a particular form of church order: thus a tract produced by one Community Church says, 'Restoration may be a new word to many, but it is simply the heart of God reaching out to touch and change the hearts of men and women;' however, it goes on

to affirm that 'the Community Church is totally committed to restoring God's Biblical order to life and worship in the local church'.

18 The Journal of George Fox, in *Quaker Spirituality*, ed D V Steere, SPCK, 1984, p 79.

19 C K Barrett, *Church, Ministry, & Sacraments in the New Testament*, Paternoster, Exeter, 1985; R E Brown, *The Churches the Apostles Left Behind*, Paulist Press, N York, 1984.

Notes to chapter two: Clericalism

1 R S Thomas, *Selected Poems 1946–1968*, Granada, 1979, p 13f.

2 T Cartwright, quoted in J Whitgift, *Defence of the Answer to the Admonition against the Reply of Thomas Cartwright*, in Works, ed J Ayre, Parker Society, Cambridge, 1852, vol ii p 490.

3 From his poem, 'On the New Forcers of Conscience Under the Long Parliament.'

4 E Schillebeeckx, *The Church with a Human Face: A New and Expanded Theology of Ministry*, SCM, 1985, p 157.

5 See B D Reed, *The Dynamics of Religion: Process and Movement in Christian Churches*, DLT, 1979; W Carr, *The Priestlike Task: A Model for Training and Developing the Church's Ministry*, SPCK, 1985.

6 *The Final Report of the Anglican-Roman Catholic International Commission*, CTS/SPCK, 1982, pp 30,40f; *Baptism, Eucharist and Ministry*, Faith and Order Paper No 111, WCC, Geneva, 1982, pp 20, 23.

7 H Kraemer, *A Theology of the Laity*, Lutterworth, 1958, p 63.

Notes to chapter three: Cultic religion

1 W Carr, op cit, p 27.

Notes to chapter four: Institutionalism

1 S Weil, *Waiting on God*, Collins Fount Paperbacks, 1977, pp 19, 21.

2 *General Synod Report of Proceedings* (July 1981 Group of Sessions), vol 12 no 2, p 496.

3   L J Francis, *Rural Anglicanism: A Future for Young Christians?*, Collins, 1985, p 12.

Notes to chapter five: The gospel community

1   Cf. E P Sanders: 'Jesus himself looked to a new age, and therefore he viewed the institutions of this age as not final, and in that sense not adequate. He was not, however, a reformer;' in *Jesus and Judaism*, SCM, 1985, p 269.

2   C K Barrett, op cit, p 13.

3   A Richardson, *An Introduction to the Theology of the New Testament*, SCM, 1958, p 284.

4   Ibid, p 310.

5   E.g. Mt 26:28; Mk 10:45; 14:24; Lk 22:20; Jn 1:29; Acts 8:32–35; Rom 3:25; 1 Cor 11:25; 2 Cor 5:20; Gal 1:4; Eph 1:7; Col 1:19; 1 Pet 1:18f; 1 Jn 1:7; 4:10; Rev 1:5.

6   Another Greek word, *mysterion*, which in paganism had a cultic significance and in the fourth century came to be applied to the Christian sacraments, is nowhere in the New Testament used to describe Christian worship.

7   Cf. R Banks: 'Since all places and times have now become the venue for worship, Paul cannot speak of Christians assembling in church *distinctively* for this purpose. They are already worshipping God, acceptably or unacceptably, in whatever they are doing. While this means that when they are in church they are worshipping as well, it is not worship but something else that marks off their coming together from everything else that they are doing.' In *Paul's Idea of Community: The Early House Churches in their Historical Setting*, Paternoster, Exeter 1980, p 91f.

Notes to chapter six: Leadership in the gospel community

1   E P Sanders, op cit, p 102, thinks the number twelve was symbolic, or at any rate variations in membership made it impossible to identify precisely twelve.

2   J D G Dunn, *Jesus and the Spirit: A Study of the Religious and Charismatic Experience of Jesus and the First Christians as Reflected in the New Testament*, SCM, 1975, p 274; cf. also pp 180ff.

3   ARCIC *Final Report*, p 83.

4   Dunn, op cit, p 182.

5 D Prior, *Bedrock: A Vision for the Local Church*, Hodder, 1985, p 119.

6 Op cit, p 25.

7 Dunn, op cit, p 360.

8 E T by H Bettenson in *The Later Christian Fathers*, Oxford, 1970, p 175f.

9 Op cit, p 23.

10 Op cit, p 36.

11 Ibid, p 41.

12 Op cit, p 22.

13 M Thurian, *Priesthood & Ministry: Ecumenical Research*, Mowbray, E T 1983, p 54.

14 E.g. Acts 18:26; 21:9; Rom. 16:1–6, 12f; 1 Cor. 1:11; 11:5; 16:19; Col. 4:15.

15 Letter from Cardinal Willebrands to the Archbishop of Canterbury, dated 17.6.1986. The logical allegory of the doctrine that the priesthood must be male to represent Christ is that those who receive the sacrament must be female to represent the church!

16 The arguments advanced from 1 Cor: 14:34f and 1 Tim. 2:11–15 against the leadership ministry of women are not only contradicted by NT practice (see refs in note 14 above) but also depend upon a use by Paul of particular rabbinic interpretations of OT Scripture which he elsewhere interprets in a different manner. Thus it is not correct to conclude that Eve was more responsible for sin than Adam (cf. Rom. 5:12; 1 Cor. 15:22), or that relationships which apply within the married state between husbands and wives should govern all relationships between men and women.

Notes to chapter seven: The changing scene

1 Kraemer, op cit, pp 64, 177.

2 P Minear, *Images of the Church in the New Testament*, 1960, p 257.

3 M Hodge, *Non-Stipendiary Ministry in the Church of England*, CIO Publishing, 1983, pp 30ff.

4 A T Hanson, *The Pioneer Ministry*, 1961, p 108.

5 *Ministry in the Seventies*, ed C Porthouse, Falcon Books, 1970, p 91.

6   E Roberts, *Partners and Ministers*, Falcon Books, 1972, pp 18ff.

7   Op cit, pp. 112–9 'Local ordained ministry is exercised within the same orders of ministry as other priests and deacons: the difference lies not in the ordination but in the process of selection and training, and of appointment and function of those whose call is to minister within the leadership team of their own local church.'

8   *The Pattern of the Church*, Lutterworth, 1963, p 137.

9   P M Miller, *Equipping for Ministry*, Central Tanganyika Press, 1969, p 47.

10 V J Donovan, *Christianity Rediscovered*, SCM, 1982, p 144f.

11 S B Clark, *Building Christian Communities*, Ave Maria Press, 1972, pp 141, 110.

12 H Kung, *Why Priests?*, Collins (Fontana), 1972, pp 54–67.

13 Concilium, *The Right of the Community to a Priest*, ed E Schillebeeckx and J-B Metz, no 133, March 1980, p 123.

14 *Renew*, the Newsletter of the Catholic Renewal Movement, March 1984.

15 K Rahner, *The Shape of the Church to Come*, SPCK, 1974, p 110.

16 *Baptism, Eucharist and Ministry*, p 27; *Final Report*, pp 31, 34.

17 J M Barnett, *The Diaconate – A Full and Equal Order*, Seabury Press, N York, 1981, p 147.

18 Ibid, p 187.

19 The Seven are not described as deacons in Acts 6, except insofar as they are to 'deacon tables' while the apostles attend to 'deaconing the word'. Some scholars see them as elders, since elders appear later in Acts at Jerusalem without any mention of their appointment (15:4). Tradition was so strong that they were deacons that in 315 AD a canon was passed forbidding the church in any one town to have more than seven deacons.

20 James Hurley argues convincingly in *Men and Women in Biblical Perspective*, IVP, 1981, p 230, that 1 Tim 3:8–13 implies both male and female deacons.

21 G W H Lampe in *Service in Christ – Essays Presented to Karl Barth on his 80th Birthday*, Epworth, 1966, p 49.

Notes to chapter eight: How some churches have established corporate leadership.

1 In a Team Ministry, a single benefice comprising one or more parishes is served by a Rector and one or more Team Vicars who share the 'cure of souls' and may have other lay or ordained ministers who share in 'the pastoral care'. There is usually an elected Team Council, and a separate District Council for each congregation.

2 A Parochial Church Council must have a Standing Committee of at least five members: the Minister and Churchwardens *ex officio*, and at least two others elected by the PCC, very often in practice the Secretary and Treasurer because Standing Committee business has normally been seen as primarily financial and administrative.

3 Many people used the term '*primus inter pares*' (first among equals) to describe the position.

Notes to chapter nine: Lessons of corporate leadership

1 A Russell, *The Clerical Profession*, SPCK, 1980, p 294f.

2 J King, article in *The Church of England Newspaper*, 6 Jan 1984.

3 A Parish Audit is a process whereby a congregation assesses the condition of the neighbourhood in which it is set, examines its own life and priorities, and in the light of this exercise makes appropriate plans for its mission strategy. Various ways in which this can be done are described in Appendix A of *Faith in the City*, and in *Mission Audit*, published by the Board of Mission and Unity, CIO Publishing.

4 Y Congar, *Lay People in the Church*, Geoffrey Chapman, 1959, p 361.

5 D Watson, *You are my God*, Hodder & Stoughton, 1983, p 164.

6 It appears that some House Churches which have hitherto insisted on a wholly male eldership have recently changed their position.

7 Op. cit. p 152.

8 D Wasdell, *Divide and Conquer*, Urban Church Project Workpaper No 2, 1974, p 24.

9   *Life and Work: The Record of the Church of Scotland*, Jan
    1985, p 15.

Notes to chapter ten: Clarifying the vision

1   *Faith in the City*, p 66.
2   E Gibbs, *I Believe in Church Growth*, Hodder &
    Stoughton, 1981, pp 380–4.
3   For a survey of training opportunities see the chapter by
    M Birchall in *Hope for the Church of England?* ed. G
    Reid, Kingsway, 1986.
4   Research is needed at the sort of level undertaken by
    Towler and Coxon, mainly between 1962 and 1967 and
    published in 1969 under the title, *The Fate of the Anglican
    Clergy*, Oxford.

Index

Index of Reports and Publications quoted